CRE🏠TIVE
HOMEOWNER®

design ideas for
Basements

Wayne Kalyn

CREATIVE HOMEOWNER®, Upper Saddle River, New Jersey

DESIGN IDEAS FOR BASEMENTS

SENIOR EDITOR	Kathie Robitz
EDITOR	Lisa Kahn
GRAPHIC DESIGNERS	Maureen Mulligan, Kathryn Wityk
PHOTO RESEARCHER	Stan Sudol
PHOTO COORDINATOR	Robyn Poplasky
JUNIOR EDITOR	Jennifer Calvert
DIGITAL IMAGING SPECIALIST	Frank Dyer
INDEXER	Schroeder Indexing Services
COVER DESIGN	Maureen Mulligan, Kathryn Wityk
COVER PHOTOGRAPHY	(all) Olson Photographic, LLC

CREATIVE HOMEOWNER

VICE PRESIDENT AND PUBLISHER	Timothy O. Bakke
ART DIRECTOR	David Geer
MANAGING EDITOR	Fran J. Donegan

Current Printing (last digit)
10 9 8 7 6 5 4 3

Design Ideas for Basements, Second Edition
Library of Congress Control Number: 2008921441
ISBN-10: 1-58011-424-5
ISBN-13: 978-1-58011-424-0

Manufactured in the United States of America

CREATIVE HOMEOWNER®
A Division of Federal Marketing Corp.
24 Park Way
Upper Saddle River, NJ 07458
www.creativehomeowner.com

Planet Friendly Publishing
✔ Made in the United States
✔ Printed on Recycled Paper
Text: 10%   Cover: 10%
Learn more: www.greenedition.org

GREEN EDITION

At Creative Homeowner we're committed to producing books in an earth-friendly manner and to helping our customers make greener choices.

Manufacturing books in the United States ensures compliance with strict environmental laws and eliminates the need for international freight shipping, a major contributor to global air pollution.

And printing on recycled paper helps minimize our consumption of trees, water, and fossil fuels. *Design Ideas for Basements* was printed on paper made with 10% post-consumer waste. According to the Environmental Defense Fund Paper Calculator, by using this innovative paper instead of conventional papers we achieved the following environmental benefits:

Trees Saved: 23
Water Saved: 10,571 gallons
Solid Waste Eliminated: 642 pounds
Greenhouse Gas Emissions Eliminated: 2,195 pounds

For more information on our environmental practices, please visit us online at www.creativehomeowner.com/green

Dedication

To my son, Scott Richard,
and daughter, Holly Jean—
the joys of my life.

Contents

RIGHT This light-filled, casual basement space invites relaxation and a good conversation over a cup of tea.

Do you need more living space? Do your domestic dreams include a home office, a deluxe media room, or perhaps a downstairs hangout for wild and crazy teens? Look no further than beneath your feet. That's right, your humble basement.

Transforming your basement into attractive, livable space can increase the value of your home and enrich your life. Fortunately, the job is easier and less expensive than you might think. In most cases, even a very ambitious project costs only a fraction of what you would spend to build an addition. Estimates for building aboveground aver-

Introduction

age about $150 a square foot; remodeling a basement, on the other hand, usually costs only $75 per square foot—that's a savings of 50 percent. The lower cost shouldn't surprise you. After all, a basement is fully enclosed and already comes with walls, a floor, and a ceiling. There's no need to break ground for an addition in order to have that hobby room, spare bath, or extra bedroom.

This book is all you need to come up with inspiration and know-how to meet your family's ever-changing and ever-growing needs for more space and greater comfort. After reading it, you'll never look at your basement the same way again.

LEFT This posh basement living room relies on tailored furniture, gleaming silver and glassware, and neutral colors, such as tan, cream, and chocolate for its sophisticated ambiance.

BELOW Expansive, custom wood cabinetry in an ivory finish provides complete storage and display space needed in this basement home office.

OPPOSITE This tiny half bath ramps up its good looks and functionality, thanks to an oversized mirror, wall cabinet, and elegant wall sconces.

These days, homeowners are demanding more living, working, and storage space. The space available in your basement can fulfill many of these requirements. There are many creative ways to redesign a basement to suit your family's needs. For example, each week you spend more time than you'd care to think about cleaning up the family wardrobe. Why not take some of the grunt out of the work by creating an efficient, well-equipped laundry room? Mudrooms, once a dark alcove for dirty boots and wet coats, have evolved into multipurpose landing pads. And who couldn't use a few extra closets and shelves?

Laundry & Storage

▎ laundry rooms ▎ mudrooms ▎
▎ storage ideas ▎

Laundry rooms these days don't have to look dull. Use color, lighting, and cheerful accessories to create a warm ambiance.

laundry rooms

Laundry rooms have caught up with the rest of the house in decor and personality. Laminate faux-wood flooring is a great way to get the look of hardwood without the worry of moisture damage. Other options are no-wax or resilient flooring, or ceramic tile, all of which come in a wide range of colors. You might also consider bringing the outside in by installing exterior brick pavers.

Color is the least expensive way to make a big impact. Semigloss paint and wallpaper are easy to clean and stand up to humidity. Try dressing up your room with a custom-painted design on one wall, or use a mirror on the wall opposite a window to fill your space with more natural light.

Counter space can be the key to spending less time on the laundry. You'll be able to treat stains and fold clothes faster. Laminates make ideal countertop surfaces in the laundry room. They are durable and easy to clean, and they come in many patterns and colors. Some homeowners take cues from their kitchens and add granite and natural stone countertops to dress up the space.

If you have the luxury of creating a laundry room near a basement window, by all means do. The natural light will almost make you whistle while you work. An overhead fixture will suffice in a small laundry room. Task lighting will brighten work surfaces, accent any artwork in your space, and help you see what you're doing when treating clothing stains or sewing on a button. Consider installing under-cabinet or recessed lighting to illuminate work, or hang a pendant fixture over the folding table.

You can upgrade a laundry room into a state-of-the-art laundry center. Install drying cabinets that dry a wool sweater in a few hours or a clothes-care valet system that removes wrinkles in 30 minutes.

LEFT Designing a laundry room near a bank of windows brightens the space, which includes generous countertops for sorting and folding clothes.

OPPOSITE Add decorative elements to cheer up the space. Here, a clothesline theme painted on the wall and carried over to the shade adds a charming, whimsical touch.

bright idea

green machines

Front-loading washers save energy and water. They spin clothes faster than top-loading models, which makes them more efficient at extracting water. As a result, it takes less time to dry clothing.

ABOVE Under-cabinet lighting provides ample illumination for tasks, and handsome stone flooring delivers good looks while resisting damage from water spills.

RIGHT Laundry rooms can be designed into compact spaces. Here, a washer-dryer combination, a small sink, and custom cabinets save space and add convenience.

OPPOSITE This laundry room makes use of every inch of space. A sink for soaking clothes is tucked into a corner, and a clothes pole is set above the counter.

small space ideas for the laundry

▮ A fold-down ironing board stores away when not in use; or a folding arm swivels out of your way when you aren't hanging clothes.

▮ Miniature rolling laundry carts can be neatly tucked away in a corner or between the washer and dryer.

▮ Stackable washers and dryers maximize space in a small laundry room.

▮ Splurge on a new floor in one afternoon by installing a single box of self-adhesive resilient tiles.

▮ Bold color helps brighten your small space. Choose paint and wallpaper colors that hide scuff marks.

▮ Hang small garage racks on the walls. These keep clutter and laundry products up and out of the way.

▮ Mount kitchen-style cabinets above the washer and dryer to conceal cleaning products, tools, and storage containers.

▮ Place a small receptacle for lint removal on a shelf, rather than using a larger trash bin that wastes precious floor space.

BELOW This decorative laundry room is anything but utilitarian. A large wooden chest, fabric window treatment, and wall art provide eye-pleasing accents.

RIGHT A freestanding his-and-her wardrobe, complete with monogrammed doors, holds freshly cleaned clothes straight from the dryer.

OPPOSITE Warm up a laundry room with color, and add eye appeal with pattern. Here, the golden tones of the walls and geometric patterned floor create a distinctive look.

the "**f**amily **s**tudio"

Laundry facilities can be incorporated handsomely into a basement room that is designed for a multitude of needs and activities. Stock or semicustom kitchen cabinetry can hide front-loading washers and dryers, hanging racks, ironing equipment, hampers, and laundry products when they are not in use. The illustration, right, shows one major appliance manufacturer's suggestion for creating a "family studio" outfitted for multitasking. It features exercise equipment, a TV, and a mini-kitchen. You can work out, watch the news, heat up a snack for the kids, or brew a fresh pot of coffee while you're getting the laundry washed and folded.

© Stephen Fuller, Inc.

laundry rooms can be designed for multitasking

mudrooms

Mudrooms are a cross between utility rooms and walk-in closest. They're a place to store and house outerwear, boots, sports gear, and anything else you need when you go outdoors. You can create a good mudroom even in a tight space. The floor in a mudroom should be durable and slip-resistant. Textured rubber or ceramic or stone tile are all good choices. Choosing a dark color for the floor will help camouflage dirt. A couple of doormats—one stationed outside made of flexible bristles or rubber to brush off dirt, and a water-absorbing one inside—can reduce muck tracked into the basement.

When it comes to wallcoverings, vinyl wallpaper will protect walls, is easy to clean, and adds color and pattern to a room.

Include seating in your mudroom. You'll need a comfortable, sturdy place to sit while pulling off shoes, boots, or skates. Benches and stools are more stable than chairs. A built-in bench or window seat, hinged at the top, can provide ample space for storage of off-season coats and footwear.

Today's mudrooms function as far more than a space to take off your boots. They handle a multitude of household activities, including sorting mail, hanging car keys, and setting down groceries. When it comes to storage, hooks, cubbies, bins, and baskets—all located at child level—will hold the kids' items. Color-coding storage areas for each member of the family keeps things in order.

Specialized bins and hangers for sports gear are designed to hold oddly shaped equipment such as racquets and mitts. Prevent pet leashes from tangling by hanging them from ordinary cup hooks. A corkboard hung on the wall can help organize information and schedules. Add counter space for sorting mail and a boot tray for soggy footwear.

OPPOSITE LEFT This combination mudroom-laundry room features a large sink for bathing the family pet or cleaning off dirty boots and clothes before dropping them into the washer.

OPPOSITE RIGHT Under-the-counter compartments hold all kinds of items—from shoes to book bags—in the mudroom, so kids can grab them as they head out the door.

RIGHT In this combination mudroom/laundry room, cabinets with mesh inserts allow wet clothes to dry without using up precious floor space.

ABOVE You can create a wall of storage behind bifold doors. Here, narrow shelves make a perfect fit for soaps and toiletries, while linens and blankets are tucked into larger shelves below.

RIGHT TOP These easy-to-install shelves free up plenty of space.

Because basements tend to be long, running the length of the house, a standard storage solution is to devote one wall to a series of closets that can house everything from out-of-season clothes to sports equipment. Use every inch of vertical space when planning shelving. Closets outfitted with wooden louver doors look handsome and allow air to circulate. When buying a shelving system, choose one that is adjustable so that you can reconfigure the shelves as your needs change. Recessed shelves built into the walls add storage without extending into living space.

To maximize living space in your home, create a dedicated storage room. Instead of using valuable wall space in a small basement, design a room that will hold all of your stuff and

storage ideas

then some. Don't forget about the back of the storage-room door. Hooks can be useful, or use an over-the-door shoe organizer for smaller items.

Make use of the area under the basement stairs. Often forgotten about and rarely used, the space under the stairs can be fashioned into a cabinet with doors or fitted with recessed shelving.

Basement storage accessories should be tailored to provide maximum access, ventilation, and moisture resistance. Because basements can be damp, metal shelving and cabinetry protect possessions better than wooden alternatives; plastic bins, in turn, protect better than cardboard boxes. If you are using plastic tubs for storing clothes, make sure that the bin is not airtight, as clothing needs some ventilation. If you do store in cardboard boxes, don't stack them—always leave space for air circulation.

If you have created a bedroom in the basement, don't forget about the area under the bed. Buy storage boxes designed to fit under the box spring. Some are on wheels or glide on a track. These are great for storing linens and seasonal items.

LEFT Handsome wood storage chests in this basement's walk-in closet resemble fine furniture.

RIGHT The homeowner makes elegant use of the long basement walls that run the length of the house with wood shelving that flanks a built-in chest for seating and storage.

organizing a clothes closet

▌ **Segment closet space** with a variety of shelves, cubby-holes, and clothes rods set at different heights.

▌ **Sort through your wardrobe,** grouping items of similar length together to determine rod heights. At 64 inches, overcoats and bathrobes use up the most vertical space when hung from a rod. Next come trousers hung by the cuff, at 48 to 56 inches, followed by shirts, jackets, and blazers.

▌ **Organize your closet by how often items are used.** Put everyday work clothes in the middle where they are easily reached, and use the corners for out-of-season clothes.

▌ **Use bins on high shelves,** roll-out boxes on the floor, and even a third closet pole (if the ceiling is over 9 feet high) for storing items you don't use all the time.

▌ **Hanging rods that hook over existing rails** don't require a power drill and create instant extra room for shorter clothing.

▌ **Install a valet rod or hook outside the closet** to hang clothes just back from the dry cleaners.

RIGHT This walk-in wardrobe closet uses see-through plastic containers, shelving, and drawers to store clothes. A mirror and a seat are convenient additions.
▌
OPPOSITE The hardwood flooring not only warms up this walk-in closet, but it also blends in beautifully with the shoe rack, chest of drawers—even the wooden hangers.

custom cabinets use every square inch of space

OPPOSITE Under-the-stairs drawers are a smart way to store an array of items.

LEFT Storage space can be seamlessly hidden behind a series of doors that look like wood paneling when closed.

BELOW This under-the-stairs closet blends into the rest of the room because of its handsome wood molding.

BOTTOM These handy drawers and decorative recessed nook are artfully arranged into an eye-catching geometric pattern.

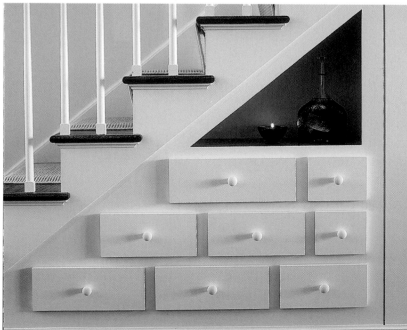

These days, homeowners are converting part, or all, of their basements into home gyms or game rooms. Dedicating space to a home gym is a wise investment. Studies show that you will exercise regularly when you have the room and a wide range of equipment at your fingertips. A 10 × 12-foot space with a 7- or 8-foot-high ceiling can accommodate two pieces of cardio equipment, a weight bench, and dumbbells. Some spaces can even handle a compact lap pool. The basement is also a perfect place for a game room, where you can play pool with friends or enjoy an evening of video or arcade games with the family.

Exercise & Game Rooms

▌ home-fitness centers ▌
▌ game rooms ▌

An ideal home gym is designed with enough space for all kinds of equipment, ample lighting, and amenities such as a flat-screen TV.

ABOVE Durable rubber flooring is easy on the feet and simple to clean.

RIGHT An exercise room should have a mix of cardio and strength-training machines.

FAR RIGHT When planning a gym in the basement, be sure the ceilings are at least 7 ft. high.

OPPOSITE RIGHT A neutral palette and overhead lighting brighten this home gym.

home-fitness centers

A drive to the local health club takes time that many of us don't have. Why not just walk down a flight of stairs to your own gym, which is open 24 hours a day, 7 days a week?

Concrete-slab floors found in most basements support heavy workout machines, but they are hard to stand on for long periods of time. You want to make sure the floor finish is durable, easy to clean, and soft underfoot. Resilient flooring—such as vinyl, linoleum, cork, and rubber—is the best choice. Vinyl or rubber tiles that are at least ⅛ inch thick are a practical and inexpensive option; they offer more protection and cushion than carpeting and are maintenance free—a few swipes of a damp rag will clean them.

Plan your gym in a section of the basement that has several operable windows. During warm weather, opening windows allows fresh air in a room that can quickly get stuffy and stale. If windows are not an option, include a large overhead fan in the design. A standing oscillating fan, or a model on a rolling stand, can help curb the heat.

Neutral and warm whites on the walls will make the gym feel brighter and more spacious. Lightweight, shatterproof acrylic mirror panels hung on the walls will reflect natural light and enable you to check out your form while strength-training.

Many people like a little entertainment to take the boredom out of their exercise routine. Integrate wiring from your media into your gym layout so you can listen to music while working out. Flush-mounted speakers in the ceiling or in the four corners of the room provide rich sound without getting in the way of your gym equipment. Fix a TV on a ceiling-mounted corner bracket so you can view the set from anywhere in the room.

mirrors in a home gym visually expand a space

ABOVE Crown molding and wide baseboards give this space a formal feel.

ABOVE RIGHT Large mirror panels allow you to check your form while exercising.

RIGHT The open design of this basement gym can accommodate the whole family.

OPPOSITE Position a TV so that everyone can view it as they work out.

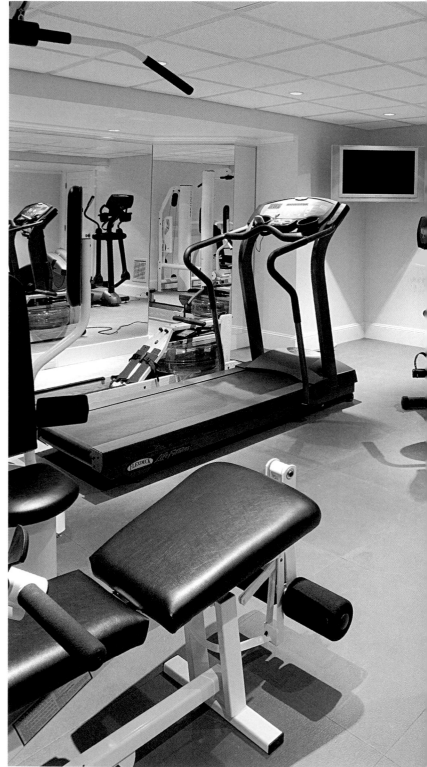

bright idea

leave room

Factor in enough space between machines to avoid banging your arms and legs. There should be a minimum of 30 inches between pieces of exercise equipment.

lap pools

Many homeowners are installing lap pools in their home gyms in addition to, or as an alternative to, treadmills and stair-steppers. Lap pools require a minimal amount of space—the most compact version is 7 x 14 feet—because a current generated by a motor keeps you swimming in place. The result is a river-like current that can be adjusted from a gentle flow to a racer's pace simply by turning a knob.

Manufacturers make ground versions and freestanding models. The basement is an ideal space for either type: plumbing and electrical services are centrally located and easily accessible

there. In addition, the concrete-slab floor can support a free-standing pool filled with water.

The width, length, and depth of the lap pool can be tailored to your basement's dimensions. The newest generation of lap pools is energy efficient and easy to maintain. You can add 6 inches of insulation to keep in the heat, as well as a retractable cover to prevent much of the humidity and heat from dampening the basement. Regular maintenance will keep the water crystal clear. You can customize lap pools with lights and an under-water mirror for checking your swimming technique.

OPPOSITE In this walk-out base-ment, windows and doors let the out-doors into the pool room.

ABOVE A roomy alcove with comfortable seating invites guests to kick back after a swim.

LEFT A panel of mirrors and large windows make this exercise room in a walk-out basement appear even larger than it is.

game rooms

Basements have everything you need to create a dedicated game room: electrical service, physical space, and especially privacy. Make sure you take time in the planning stages. You'll need to decide how much space you have to devote to your game room and what kinds of games you want to put in it.

Game room furnishings have expanded over the years. With so many options these days, you are no longer limited to just a pool table or dartboard. Consider installing a bar or a jukebox and different types of games, such as foosball or ping pong. Many pool table manufacturers have matching accessories for the table, including bars, spectator chairs, game table chairs, pub tables, and a matching entertainment center for a television and videogame console.

If you're looking for a card table for your weekend poker game, you have almost unlimited options, from full-size portable tables with room for up to 10 players to tables that fold up and can be stored in a closet. If you want the table to be the center of attention, formal pedestal card tables are designed in oak, cherry, and a variety of other hardwoods.

If your gaming preferences go beyond Texas Holdem, look into casino tables that allow you to play roulette, craps, checkers, chess, backgammon, and poker simply by flipping the table top. They also contain storage compartments for chips, game pieces, and other paraphernalia.

Creating an arcade space, complete with pinball machines and other arcade games, has never been easier. Manufacturers make game cabinets that contain 80 classic games and feature two controllers, a track ball, and a 25-inch monitor. There are even video arcade centers, which use a projector and PC combo to offer a video jukebox and home theater in one system.

TOP LEFT Almost any arcade game you played in your younger days is available for the home.

LEFT A handsome stone fireplace and wood floor warm up this inviting home arcade parlor.

OPPOSITE Bold colors, dramatic lighting, and a tray ceiling create eye appeal.

pool tables

Pool tables have become increasingly popular center-pieces in a basement game room. Standard sizes of billiard tables range from 44 x 96 inches for an 8-foot table from bumper to bumper, to 56 x 112 inches for a 10-foot table.

Pool tables come in many styles, including European, traditional, Arts & Crafts, casual, and competition. If your space is limited, you might want to try two-in-one or three-in-one tables. The two-in-one is a pool table with a reversible top so it can serve as a dining table or card table. The three-in-one includes bumper pool in its base.

Pool tables vary in price. At the lower end, there are mass-market, assemble-it-yourself tables for under $1,000. At the high end, professional tables can run into five figures.

OPPOSITE BELOW Customize a game room to your tastes. Here, a paneled wood ceiling and walls add handsome architectural details.

LEFT A wall of windows dressed with wood shutters allows natural light to fill this room, but provide privacy when the shutters are closed. Built-in banquette seating takes up little floor space.

BELOW A suite of upholstered barrel chairs and a small table provide a comfortable spot for conversation at the other end of this room.

▏▎▍▌ there's a wide range of furniture styles for a game room ▌▍▎▏

ABOVE A full bar, complete with beverage center and a wine cooler, blends nicely with this modern room. Note the Arts and Crafts styling of the pool table.

OPPOSITE TOP The owners' collection of framed prints add personality to the space. Overhead lighting and wall sconces brighten the room, which has little natural light.

OPPOSITE BOTTOM The kitchenette beyond the snack bar is a convenient feature, especially during small parties.

bright idea

play it safe

If children spend time in the game room, play it safe and install an electronic dartboard that doesn't have sharp-tipped darts rather than the real thing.

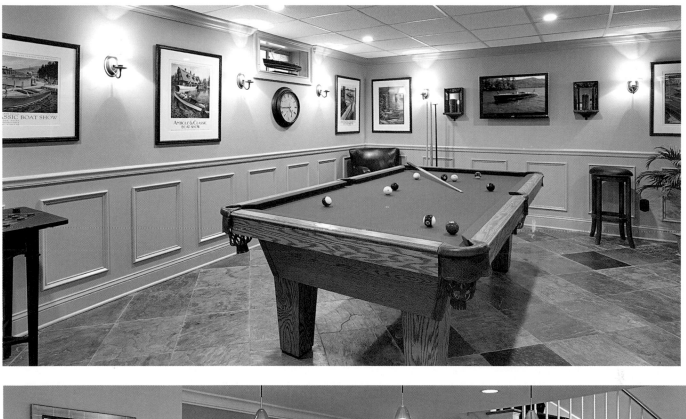

video games & arcades

If you like to play video games loudly, soundproof walls and carpeted floors will keep the noise from leaking into other parts of the house. Put lights on a dimmer to prevent washing out the vibrant colors on the screen.

Most arcade games are available for home use these days. Primary lighting should emanate from the game's screen and marquee. Strong overhead lighting can produce glare. Add a jukebox to the arcade—companies offer reproductions as well as souped-up digital models.

OPPOSITE TOP Racy red is a lively accent, especially when it's paired with neutral walls and black-painted wood.

OPPOSITE BOTTOM Bench-style leather seating is a practical addition.

BELOW Fabric-paneled walls and thick carpeting help to muffle loud noise.

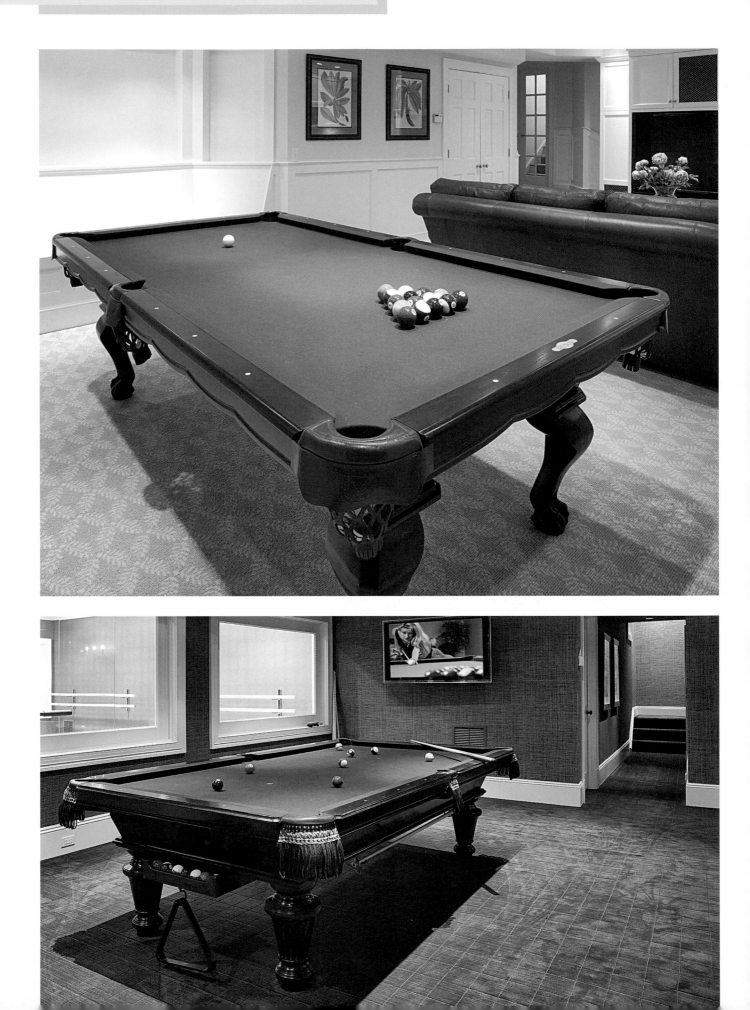

OPPOSITE TOP These days, pool tables come in a range of styles that fit the decor of any room. Here, claw-and-ball legs strike a formal English note.

OPPOSITE BOTTOM Pool tables come in different finishes, as well. This mahogany color looks rich and masculine.

BELOW Whether playing backgammon, poker, or another game, the table is the focal point of the room. Soft, warm lighting above the table and around the room enhance the physical comfort and mood of this space.

3

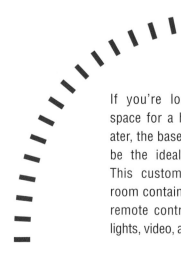

When it comes to the basement, a remodeler's first inclination is often to carve out space for a media room. That's a smart move. An entertainment room outfitted with one or more video-game consoles, a big-screen TV, and digital music components taps into a basement's natural assets: darkness, separation from everyday household activities, and shape. What's more, with the advent of more affordable media equipment, home theaters are being incorporated into even the most modest of finished basements. A successful home theater depends more on careful space planning and layout than anything else.

Media Rooms

I media equipment I
I it's show time I

If you're looking for space for a home theater, the basement may be the ideal location. This custom-designed room contains a digital remote control for the lights, video, and sound.

ABOVE You can create a home theater that is functional and beautiful. Here speakers are aesthetically arranged on the ceiling and walls for the ultimate listening experience.

OPPOSITE When using a front-projection system, make sure that the ceiling is high enough so that people won't bang their heads. An ideal distance is 8 feet or higher.

bright idea

hassle free

You can also buy a home theater in a box. It contains almost everything you need for a basic setup. Just unpack it, and plug in the cord.

High-definition TV (HDTV) has taken television to the next level. If you are going to the trouble and expense of creating a home theater—even a modest one—in your basement, it's worth investing in an HDTV-compatible model. HDTV is a digital signal that carries a more detailed image and is encoded with surround-sound information.

So what are your options? Newer flat-screen cathode-ray tube (CRT) sets eliminate the distortion caused by the curved edges of older models.

Slimmed-down flat-panel plasma TVs and LCD screens provide brilliant colors, better contrast and resolution, and greater viewing angles. Rear-projection TVs have the largest screen of any of the above models. The screen size of a rear-projection TV can be 82 inches—and can be viewed in natural light without sacrificing picture quality.

media equipment

Front-projection systems have a separate screen, which can either drop down from the ceiling or remain fixed on the wall, and a projector that is mounted at ceiling height across the room from the screen. It's akin to a movie-theater system.

DVD players are at the heart of today's home-theater systems. Spend a little more, if you can, on a progressive-scan DVD player, which creates a smoother picture than traditional models. For convenience, get a player with a disc changer.

Digital video recorders (DVRs) work much like personal computers, recording programming from cable or a satellite dish onto a hard drive. Or you can burn copies of a movie or television program using an integrated DVD recorder.

| | | | | | | **buy a remote with an illuminated keypad** | | | | | | | | | |

bright idea

sound advice

Wattage is a good indicator of how loud a speaker can play without distortion. Choose speakers that are closely matched to your receiver's watts-per-channel rating. Don't worry about a small difference; to double the volume, you need ten times the power.

OPPOSITE A front-projection system like this one requires professional installation, but the image quality can be unbeatable.

LEFT To watch movies in their original wide-screen format, you'll need a TV with a rectangular shape 16:9 aspect ratio.

BELOW Special architectural details, plush velvet seating, and dramatic low lighting replicate some of the glamour of Hollywood in the 1930s.

consulting a pro

If you want the ultimate in home-theater sight and sound, have a pro design the room and install the components. These days, home-theater designers use acoustic software to configure the optimal dimensions for the space and determine screen and speaker placement, as well as lighting and seating needs. When the design is complete, you can take a virtual tour of your home theater before any work takes place.

These professionals often recommend acoustical treatment of the space before equipment and furniture is purchased. Acoustical engineering typically consists of three types of surfaces: absorptive, diffusive, and reflective. A home theater requires the right mixture of all three in order to produce a lush sound similar to that of a movie theater. Designers also configure noise-control solutions to prevent sound from traveling throughout the house.

A home-theater expert can design a basement media room that conceals all wiring and integrates speakers, components, lighting, and video for an optimal viewing and listening experience. Look for Custom Electronic Design and Installation Association (CEDIA) certification when hiring your expert.

‖‖‖‖‖‖‖ built-in features eliminate distracting clutter while

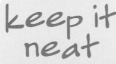

bright idea

keep it neat

Include plenty of rollout drawers in your design to hold your library of favorite discs and tapes. Leave room for future purchases, too.

OPPOSITE A deep red tone-on-tone wallcovering and wood panels are conducive to keeping reflective light low in this room.

LEFT Note the cozy seating nook for kids that was built into the wall.

BELOW LEFT AND RIGHT A frameless cabinet door and concealed hinges help to camouflage in-the-wall storage for numerous electronic components.

protecting expensive equipment IIIIIIIIIIIIIIIIIIIIIIIIIIIIIIIIII

Even the most-expensive equipment will sound its best in a properly outfitted media room. For those with a large budget, thick concrete walls with no windows, solid-core doors with yards of weatherstripping, and sound-absorbing baffles on the walls and ceiling will result in something your friends will envy. But you can create a terrific media room even if your funds are limited. Start with a space that is configured like a rectangle and can be closed off from any other area. Also, there should be as few doors and windows as possible, and the latter should be covered with thick panels or motorized curtains that close with the flick of a button on your remote. Too much light from windows increases screen glare and reduces contrast. On the other hand,

it's show time

staring at a brightly lit screen in an otherwise dark room will strain your eyes. Installing dimmer switches on fixtures will allow you to set lights at a comfortable level.

Creating a media room will also entail hooking up more than electronics. You'll need proper housing for all of the components, as well as ample storage for CDs, DVDs, and video-game cartridges. You can go the custom route, or check out the specialty cabinetry that's on the market.

Media-room cabinetry should accommodate components at eye level for easy operation. The upper and lower shelves can be reserved for lesser-used items. If you plan to build the cabinet yourself, remember that there should be "breathing room" around the components; built-in electronics need ventilation. Plus, you have to leave space in the back of the cabinet for wires, and openings to pull through any cords that have to be plugged into wall outlets. Shelving that swivels or rolls out for easy access to the components is a good idea, as is cabinetry with interior lights.

OPPOSITE If you have the budget, a custom-designed home theater can be an ideal way to utilize space in your basement.

RIGHT Integrate built-in storage for your DVD collection with housing for a big screen TV.

BELOW Seating that is designed especially for a home theater can make the most of your viewing experience.

LEFT Elevated seating allows everyone to enjoy the show.

ABOVE Built-in cup holders are a nifty convenience.

OPPOSITE Well-lit stairs are a smart safety feature.

comfortable seating

When it comes to seating in a media room, the main focus should be on functionality—enhancing your comfort and the entertainment experience. You can achieve both by furnishing the room with chairs, sectionals, and sofas that are upholstered in soft fabrics. Upholstery absorbs sound and can provide the comfort you need when watching a two-hour movie.

Choose seating that provides adequate support, without being too hard. On the other hand, an overstuffed couch that's too soft may make standing up later difficult. To accommodate personal preferences, consider more than one style of seating. You might include a couch or love seat, an easy chair, and a straight-backed chair. To recreate cinema ambiance, install movie-house-style row seating, complete with cup holders and reclining chaises.

|||||| **generally, no lamp should be brighter than the TV screen** ||

set the mood

Rather than one or two bright-light sources, install several low-level lights. Dimmers allow you to adjust lights for viewing a DVD or computer screen. Indirect illumination, such as ceiling fixtures that light the ceiling evenly or cove lighting along the tops of the walls, provides ambient light without on-screen glare. To avoid eyestrain, position light sources behind you, not between you and the screen.

ABOVE Because they don't flood the space with light, these wall sconces are a good choice for creating a comfortable atmosphere in this space.

OPPOSITE TOP When the movie is not playing, recessed ceiling fixtures provide good general illumination—and they don't take up any floor space.

OPPOSITE BOTTOM Lighting on either side of the doors brightens the exit when the show's over.

some HDTVs automatically switch to 3-D mode

OPPOSITE For movie-theater realism, look for an HDTV with built-in 3-D capabilities.

ABOVE Incorporate as much sophis-ticated equipment as possible, includ-ing speakers that can support surround sound.

ABOVE RIGHT This space includes an elevated platform for the screen. The speakers are built into the cabinet.

RIGHT The picture on a new flat screen does not have the distortions of an older curved-screen TV.

A basement is the perfect venue for kids' play and adult hobbies and crafts. In a basement play zone, kids can make more noise and mess than would probably be acceptable in the main living area. The same benefits apply to locating a crafts room in the basement. Dust, clutter, and supplies are confined to a single area, and fumes from paint or glue can be ushered out of the house by a quiet, powerful fan before they ever reach the upstairs rooms. Another valuable commodity is privacy, which will allow you the peace and quiet to complete your project or masterpiece without interruption.

Fun Spaces

▌ kids' play space ▌ hobby space ▌
▌ gathering spots ▌

A gathering spot can have it all: whimsical details, child-friendly seating, and the coziness of wall-to-wall carpeting and a hearth and fireplace.

Every house should have a space where kids can just be kids, where they can enjoy their quiet time, toss a ball, or wrestle in a pile of pillows. Kids need room to run around and play, so when planning a play area, be sure to leave much of the floor space open. Arrange furniture, storage units, and activity centers around the perimeter of the room. Furnishings should be rugged and easy to clean. Cover sharp corners on low furniture and counters. Larger items such as toy boxes, computers, or TVs on wheels or casters are easy to move, so they can be pushed out of the way. Building tables, desks, and storage into the walls or recesses adds more open floor space.

An open floor area will allow you to reconfigure the room as children grow. For instance, the play space may be able to accommodate more furniture for friends who come over to hang out, as well as the occasional sleepover.

kids' play space

Kids love nooks and crannies, so look for ways to break up the open spaces. Two easy solutions are building a kid-size room under the stairs or a platform in an alcove that can function as a stage for puppet shows, impromptu performances, or a place to serve tea. Walls should be durable in a play space; concrete walls, with rugged woodwork, are better than drywall when metal toys bang into it, and it is much easier to remove crayon from high-gloss paint than a flat finish.

Design the play space so that it has access to a window. If you can't, create a window seat by placing a bench against a wall, flanking it with storage bins, and painting a pretend window on the wall. You can also cover a section of wall with a chalkboard or chalkboard paint, dry-erase board, or tile board. Make king-size pinup boards with cork- or burlap-covered walls where kids can hang up their artwork or make collages.

OPPOSITE Kids can draw, erase, and draw again on this wall painted with special chalkboard paint.

RIGHT Don't forget to create special places in a playroom for kids to act or to even have a pretend tea party (walk-out basement shown).

BELOW The arched entrance and shuttered windows give this play room a fairytale feel.

ABOVE Built-in storage makes use of every available square inch of space and keeps all of the kids' stuff behind closed doors.

OPPOSITE Bold colors on the walls and woodwork add a touch of whimsy to the room, while bench seating and a clothes rack add convenience.

kid clutter

Storage in a play area should include a range of options, including drawers, bins, shelves, chests, and cubbies. It should be height appropriate—storage close to the floor is good for younger kids, and taller cabinets and higher shelves will work well as they grow. Clear plastic bins make it easy to find toys and put them away. You can use the space under the stairs to create a storage closet when toys and stuffed animals no longer fit on shelves or in baskets. Attach freestanding storage units to a wall to prevent them from tipping over.

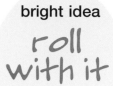

bright idea

roll with it

Rolling storage units allow kids to move them to the toys. They can also be easily wheeled outside if your basement has a walk-out area.

▮ ▮ vinyl and rubber are forgiving choices in a play area ▮ ▮ ▮ ▮ ▮ ▮ ▮ ▮

OPPOSITE This stone-pattern floor "floats" for
quick and easy installation.

▮

ABOVE The jigsaw-theme flooring is fun for kids
and comfortable to play on.

I f your hobby has been confined to a corner of the kitchen table and must be gathered up and stored away in order for you to eat, a dedicated hobby space in a remodeled basement could be just what you need.

Whether you're scrapbooking, sewing, building decoys, tying flies, or just collecting mementos of your favorite sports team, think about the work surface first. A table on wheels can be moved around as needed. A countertop peninsula allows you to see—and reach—your handiwork from three sides. A long laminate countertop permits you to spread out work that has lots of bits and pieces. Flooring should be comfortable and resistant to spills. Vinyl and laminate are easy to clean and can take the impact of rolling furniture and chairs.

hobby space

If you can, design the space near a window. It will brighten the room and let in fresh air at the same time.

Adding task lighting is very important in a hobby space; under-cabinet lighting as well as movable lights come in handy. Adjustable floor lamps are another good option. When designing the lighting, make sure you include enough outlets so that you don't need to run wires across the floor.

Storage is key. Open shelving will allow you to find what you need in a flash. Burlap or cork pinup boards on the walls can hold sketches and scraps of fabric. A wide chair rail can be used as a shallow shelf.

RIGHT This golf studio allows you to practice your game on an indoor green while playing on a virtual course.

OPPOSITE TOP A painting studio should have lots of counter space for materials and comfortable seating from which to work and admire your masterpiece.

OPPOSITE BOTTOM This music room is set off from the rest of the space with comfortable chairs and artwork. Recessed lighting brightens the room.

ABOVE A crafts studio needs workspace and storage. Here, cabinets hold lesser-used items, and open shelving keeps necessities close at hand.

OPPOSITE This cooking nook/craft studio has it all. A bright work area, small drawers and cubbies for miscellaneous items, shelves for favorite cookbooks, and a large customized cabinet for yarns, ribbon, and fabric.

craft areas

It's best to organize craft spaces around activity centers. A sewer's activity list might include areas for machine sewing, cutting, pressing, fitting, and hand finishing. Generally, L-, T-, and U-shaped spaces are more efficient than straight, in-line workspaces. A large work island in the middle of the area is another option. Be sure that tables are adjustable so you can work standing up or sitting down. A rolling table or counter with a drop-down leaf provides additional flexibility. Include storage in the activity centers, and use a mix of shelves, drawers, and cubbies.

Whether you call them family rooms or gathering spots, these are spaces where families and friends can relax, get together, and enjoy each other's company. Paying attention to design issues will help you fashion a comfortable, workable room that enhances togetherness and good times.

Plan furniture groupings to encourage both comfort and conversation, but don't crowd too much furniture in a small room, either. If the space is large, don't line the perimeter of the room with furniture, leaving a large open space in the middle. Having two or more seating areas increases the room's versatility. Group pieces around a cozy fireplace, a

gathering spots

wood-burning stove, or a flat-screen TV. Including a large round table in the space will encourage people to sit down and talk or play board games or cards.

Seating should include comfortable, durable—it will see a lot of use—and easy-to-clean upholstered pieces. If you have young children, slipcovers are a wise choice. Light, casual fabrics, such as cotton, denim, and sisal, wear well and welcome family and friends to put up their feet up and let their hair down. A sleeper sofa comes in handy when a friend or relative decides to spend the night, and a futon or two will encourage kids to nod off while watching television.

A coffee table is a must. Choose one that allows you to adjust its height for different activities and toss toys, DVDs, and the TV listings in the drawers. A laminate top is sturdy and won't show fingerprints as easily as a glass-topped table.

LEFT A gathering spot encourages everyone to do their own thing—watch television, read a book, or just kick back and relax.

OPPOSITE Include a large table with informal seating to bring everyone together. Add overhead lighting and a warm color on the mantel wall to provide a cozy feel.

RIGHT Warm up any gathering place with an electric fireplace.

BOTTOM Natural light is always a valuable addition to a family room.

OPPOSITE Throw pillows and built-in seating create a casual, inviting theme.

electric fireplaces

Electric fireplaces don't require ventilation the way traditional fireplaces do, so they can be used in a wide variety of locations and can be installed without costly home construction. In most cases, you simply plug the unit into a wall and let the heating begin. Usually, a 120-volt outlet is all that's required to provide the warmth and visual appeal of a well-tended fire. A good electric fireplace can generate up to 5,000 Btu of heat, and can be controlled with a thermostat to keep the room at a comfortable temperature. Some portable models can be easily moved from one location to another, making them a perfect choice for warming up a chilly basement bedroom or playroom.

Electric fireplaces require little maintenance and no cleanup because no soot or ash is produced. In addition, you don't have to worry about the risk of a fire caused by flying embers catching on carpet or draperies.

Because an electric fireplace does not burn real wood, how does it reproduce the lifelike quality of a fire? The "flames" you see are caused by refracted light and colored lightbulbs.

Wine cellars and martini bars have become popular amenities to add to a home, especially when it's time to finish the basement. If you're serious about wine, the basement is often an ideal location for a wine cellar because it's usually darker and cooler than the rest of the house, with levels of humidity that will prevent corks from drying out. A home bar is a great place to relax and entertain friends. There are lots of ways to make it friendly, fun, and practical. If your basement is large, you may have room for both of these spaces. Here are some ideas.

Wine Storage and Bars

❙ wine cellars ❙ wet bars ❙

Great wine must be stored properly to maintain its taste and value as an investment.

ABOVE Faux stone-painted walls, potted plants, stone-tile floors, and ornate woodwork create old Tuscan ambiance in this space.

TOP RIGHT A custom-made stained-glass window adds both beauty and privacy to the room.

RIGHT The wine cellar is separated from the rest of the basement by a wood-framed glass door.

wine cellars

Fine wine can be an investment, an indulgence, or both. A proper wine cellar will organize wines so that you can have the perfect bottle on hand for every occasion, and it will also protect your investment—well-kept wine increases in value. If you're serious about collecting, consult a wine expert during the design process to find out how different types of wine must be stored. But even if wine is simply a hobby, you'll want to create a place where you can organize bottles under the best conditions—dark (no direct sunlight) and cool. The temperature should be between 55° and 58° F at all times and the humidity level between 55 and 75 percent. Close off the area with an exterior-grade door in order to maintain those conditions precisely. If you're building a wine cellar in an unfinished basement, seal the concrete walls and floors with a vapor barrier or foam insulation before installing drywall and flooring. Porcelain tile or hardwood are good choices. You'll also need a cooling unit and possibly a drain. The cooling unit's size depends on how close the natural environment comes to the recommended wine-storage temperature and whether it is consistent year-round. Of course, check with your local building department regarding whether or not you need a permit before you begin the project.

built-in **w**ine **s**torage

Whether you have a couple of cases of your favorite California vintage or a roomful of wines from around the world, there is a storage solution for your collection. Manufacturers offer wine-rack kits in redwood and country pine, and even tasting tables that incorporate storage. Wine-storage kits come in a variety of configurations, some complete with crown and base moldings to give them a customized look. Wine cabinets are ideal for homeowners who want self-contained wine storage that blends with existing furniture and decor. A space-saving solution is a refrigerated cabinet that offers racking space and wine refrigeration in one. Custom wine-storage racks can be designed to fit the exact specifications of your basement cellar. They include sturdy systems that are earthquake resistant for oversize magnum bottles.

OPPOSITE TOP LEFT Low-voltage lighting is ideal in this space.

OPPOSITE TOP RIGHT Storing bottles with the labels facing up makes it easy to grab the right vintage.

OPPOSITE BOTTOM The geometric touches and curvilinear wine racks give this space a modern, open feel.

BELOW A bank of glass doors in this walk-out basement shows off the wine collection while sealing it off from temperature fluctuations.

RIGHT This wine cellar strikes a modern tone. Here, the cube-shape wine racks are minimal and monotone in color.

OPPOSITE Red leather banquettes in an adjoining room provide comfortable seating for tasting parties.

bright idea

super organized

Software is available to help you manage your wine inventory. There's even an online service that will do the job for you.

||||||||||||| a minimal look for the modern eonophile ||||||||

OPPOSITE An arched doorway echoes the shape of the cabinet it faces. The intricate metal-grille insert in the solid-wood door complements the elegance of the room's design.

LEFT The mosaic-tile backsplash, antiqued, chestnut-stained cabinets, exposed-apron copper sink, and the mustard-painted walls bring a French-country accent to the room.

BOTTOM An iron chandelier—a reproduction of a centuries-old candelabra—completes the look.

Old World-style details add richness to the room

bright idea
go lightly

Some experts recommend avoiding ultraviolet light entirely in a wine cellar. For good overall illumination, install IC-rated recessed canisters.

||||||||| a subterranean room that's perfect for aging wine |||

OPPOSITE TOP This room has been designed to resemble a centuries-old wine cave.

OPPOSITE BOTTOM A stone bench and an old-fashioned oak barrel are perfect for tasting events.

TOP LEFT Stone archways and columns recall the limestone walls of the natural caves in France.

ABOVE The wide-plank floor and door are important details that enhance the vintage look.

bright idea
alternative design

If you don't have enough room in your basement for built-in wall cabinets—which are important for storage—and a separate bar counter, use a bar table and bar-height chairs or stools.

OPPOSITE This well-stocked tasting area adjoins a temperature-controlled wine-storage room. The door is exterior-grade with insulated glass to keep the temperature between 55° and 58° F.

BELOW Lighting and atmosphere in this combination wine cellar and tasting room are muted to create a mellow feeling. The painted ceiling resembles aged plaster and is a perfect foil for the cool stone floor tile.

investigate different racking options

Today's wet bars suit homeowners who want an inviting and accessible space for entertaining friends and family, but who don't want to run upstairs all the time for slices of lime or those special martini and margarita glasses. The current generation of wet bars has it all—dedicated storage for liquor and glassware, built-in wine coolers, refrigerators, icemakers, kegerators, a dishwasher, a sink with running water, and even room in the plan for a plasma TV. You can have

wet bars

the bar custom designed to suit any decor, or you can buy it. Bars mostly come in wood and stainless steel. As with most furniture options, go with wood for a traditional feel or stainless steel for a modern look. Within those two choices, there is a variety of finishes and designs to fit the tastes of just about anyone. Most wet bars are designed in either a rectangular or an L shape. However, manufacturers make circular and elliptical shaped wet bars to blend in with your unique space and decor.

If you entertain large groups and require extensive preparation of food and drinks, a bar against the wall provides generous storage for liquors and glassware, as well as work space and room for a blender, a microwave, or even small kitchenette that lets you heat hors d'oeuvres. Include comfortable seating in the form of bar stools that offer good back support as well as sophisticated styling. Finally, don't forget to set a mood—use indirect, low lighting and install dimmers.

OPPOSITE TOP Well-designed cabinets take smart advantage of a corner to create a small wet bar.

OPPOSITE BOTTOM A custom-designed bar makes good use of this corner.

RIGHT Handsome cherry cabinets, a marble countertop, and ceiling tiles that resemble tin re-create the look of a turn-of-the-century saloon.

refined details have traditional appeal

bright idea

smart storage

Interior cabinet options—such as pull-out racks and drawer dividers, for example—can keep appliances or small items, such as corkscrews, handy.

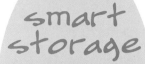

OPPOSITE TOP Handsome mahogany-stained cabinets, dark granite counters, refined tile, and elegant sconces pull the look together.

LEFT This compact design has enough storage for barware and a small wine rack. Drawers are to hold linens.

BELOW A large mirror designed to look like a window increases the sense of space. Lighting tucked behind the crown molding "lifts" the ceiling.

bright idea

just like the corner bar

Space out small thin-panel TVs around a large bar so that everybody can watch their team.

design a sports bar around your favorite team

OPPOSITE TOP Custom cabinets are beautiful and functional. Here, they provide space for everything from a large TV to speakers.

LEFT This bar has it all—plenty of storage, a wine cooler, two warming ovens, a sink, and a dishwasher.

OPPOSITE BOTTOM The large curvilinear design allows guests to socialize in groups while watching the big game.

BELOW Handsome granite countertops provide elbow room for guests and ample workspace for the bartender to prepare drinks and small snacks.

custom **c**abinetry

Custom cabinets come in oak, cherry, walnut, mahogany, and even teak. When configuring your cabinetry needs, include open shelving and glass-front cabinets to show off fancy glassware and vintage champagne or wine, as well as solid-wood doors to hide basic bar necessities. For a seamless look, consider framing under-counter refrigerators, freezer drawers, icemakers, and wine coolers with finishing panels fabricated from the same type of wood. The style of your wet bar—casual, rustic, elegant, or antique—will dictate your choices. Choose from double- or single-handle fixtures that come in bronze, brushed nickel, or stainless steel. Sinks can be as small as a single bowl or larger to accommodate dirty dishes. Some include extra workspace for cutting limes or for more serious food preparation. Don't forget the bar countertop. Choices include wood, ceramic tile, natural stone, metal, solid-surfacing, and even leather. Stone countertops are stain resistant and easy to wipe clean.

OPPOSITE TOP This intimate bar for two maximizes limited space with a graceful wraparound solid-surface countertop and built-in cabinets.

ABOVE Custom cabinetry was created for a homeowner's wine collection and features separate sections for different types of wines and vintages.

TOP RIGHT To maintain a cohesive design, all of the wood surfaces here have been stained the same honey-tone hue.

RIGHT The different heights of the countertops in this design cater to different functions.

build your own "Irish pub"

ABOVE The woodwork, wall paneling, and ceiling all help to blend this formal wood bar into the space.

ABOVE RIGHT A brass rail runs around this ornate bar to protect the rich wood from scuffing.

OPPOSITE TOP A large island contains a sink and dishwasher. Ceiling lights provide enough illumination to prepare drinks and heat snacks.

RIGHT A ledge on the wall opposite the bar is a convenient spot to rest a drink when there's a crowd.

bright idea

nice touch

A small wooden counter or shelf is a nice addition to a sit-down bar for when people want to break away from the pack.

When remodeling your basement, think beyond knotty pine paneling and fluorescent lights. The architectural details you love upstairs can help transform the space downstairs. A stairway can be dressed up with stylish handrail configurations. Use a French door for the entry to let in light and add style. If you want privacy, look for doors with blinds between the glass. Light colored glossy paints on walls can reflect light and brighten the space. Paint a faux tray ceiling or a garden window on the wall. Enhance built-in storage with decorative trim. And don't forget about the space underneath the stairs.

Architectural Elements

I neat ideas I stairways I
I it's in the details I

Use a striking balustrade and wainscoting to create drama in a room.

ABOVE Built-in cubbies and baskets for each member of the family near the entry of this basement hold miscellaneous items.

RIGHT Customized cabinetry with a coat rack is a must for a mudroom entryway.

OPPOSITE Closets with rich wood doors that are framed in trimwork fit the decor of this space.

A basement mudroom or an entry with plenty of storage can keep clutter from invading the rest of the house. There are ways to make the space both functional and stylish. A hardwood window seat topped with an upholstered cushion not only holds stuff of all shapes and sizes but also provides convenient seating when taking off and putting on boots. Built-in shelves underneath a counter provide a place for sporting equipment and backpacks, as well as a work space to clean off muddy clothes. Colorful baskets are an inexpensive storage solution that can accent the color of the walls.

neat ideas

Manufacturers offer storage systems that you can install on available wall space next to the entry door. Some include wooden drawers for small items and stainless-steel poles for hanging backpacks, handbags, and keys. Over-the-door storage systems fit on the back of a closet door and can hold coats, as well as shoes and boots. Increase the storage space in a closet by outfitting it with wooden cubbies. Paint each cubby a different color to give it some flair—or color-code several cubbies for each person in the household. Custom shelving to fit specific storage needs is always a good solution.

RIGHT This built-in storage unit holds boots, umbrellas, and outerwear, as well as leashes and toys for a treasured pet.

BOTTOM An open closet provides storage in stylish baskets on upper shelves and a comfortable spot for the family pooch to curl up for a nap.

OPPOSITE A handy bench with cubbies fits neatly under a storage shelf.

a **p**lace for **p**ets

If you have one or more pets, creating open or closed storage in the basement to store bowls, food, beds, kitty litter, and grooming tools is neater and more convenient than having them spread throughout the house. What's more, Rascal's paws won't dirty up the kitchen floor after playing outdoors.

Built-ins maximize the use of space. They can also be constructed to fit into small or oddly-shaped spaces. This is important in a basement, where nooks and crannies are often in plentiful supply.

BOTTOM LEFT Cable-like balusters give this staircase a nautical feel, echoing the photographs on the wall.

BOTTOM RIGHT The intricately shaped newel post and balusters give this stairway a Victorian feel.

OPPOSITE The stain used on these simple oak stairs highlights the wood's grain.

stairways

Stairs should set the tone for the entire basement. The treads can be clear-finished hardwood with pine risers. If sound or footing is an issue, a high-quality stair runner can be installed. If your home has a chair rail or wainscoting, the stairs can be similarly detailed. Current building codes require stairs to be constructed a minimum of 36 inches wide, allowing you to go comfortably up and down the stairs, as well as for moving furniture in and out of the space.

Stair railings are often a prominent feature of a basement, and can add flair to your downstairs space. Handrails and balusters come in a variety of styles and finishes. It is best to take your cues from the other woodwork that is in your home and any existing stairs. Balusters come in a variety of shapes. They can be made of wood for a traditional look or even decorative steel to complement modern decor.

striking railing configurations make a stylish statement

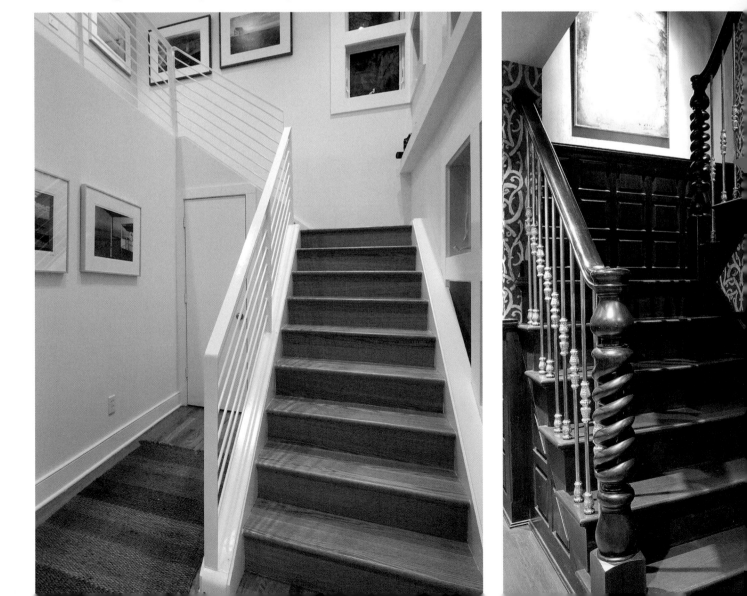

bright idea

Upstairs, downstairs

A relatively inexpensive way to make a stair railing is to build a half-wall. To protect the top of the wall, cap it with stained or painted wood.

stairway **s**tyles

Spiral stairways are not only less expensive than installing a full staircase; they also save space. Manufacturers make spiral stairs in steel, hardwoods, and a combination of these materials. Hardwood stairs come in red oak, poplar, cherry, and other handsome varieties. Steel and aluminum are available in a variety of finishes, from hot-dipped galvanized to custom color coatings. One manufacturer offers illuminated treads. For safety's sake, building codes demand specific tread and riser dimensions, and place restrictions on head-height clearance and railing placement.

BELOW This rustic-looking spiral staircase is not only eye-catching; it also works well with the wood columns and paneling, as well as the shape of the curved bar.

OPPOSITE The steel-and-wood spiral staircase creates a curvy alcove. It also picks up the shape of the iron grille leading to the wine cellar.

bright idea

lighting the way

Locate light switches so that
you can turn a light on when you
walk down or up the stairs and off
when you reach your destination.
Installing recessed fixtures
along the staircase wall
lights your way.

OPPOSITE A simple chandelier and
recessed ceiling lights offer ample
illumination on this basement
staircase.

BOTTOM LEFT The wainscoting on
the stairs, as well as the bordered
ceiling beams, are reminiscent of the
Arts and Crafts style.

BOTTOM RIGHT The lighter-hued
treads and handrails contrast smartly
with this room full of dark trim.

IIIII stairways can set the tone for the entire basement IIIIII

it's in the details

Designers and homeowners agree that the last thing anyone wants is a remodeled basement that looks and feels like—well—a basement. So pull out all of the stops when you're choosing windows, doors, and wall finishes. Wood doors perform well in the basement, provided that the space is dry and moisture is controlled. So consider making the passage from one area into another memorable by installing a door with style. Use French doors, which separate without closing off natural light. Dress them up with curtains. Use graceful louver doors to house a laundry center or a closet. Arch-shape doors or doors upholstered in fabric or decorated with a trompe l'oeil design work for a wine-cellar or cigar-room entry. Consider installing new, larger windows or additional small windows to increase light and ventilation. You can cut into the wall to add a full-size window or dig down to drop in a large window complete with a sunny well. Homeowners who have a walkout basement with one wall above grade can double or triple their natural light and ventilation by bumping out the wall to create a sunroom. Hide concrete block foundation walls behind drywall, brick or stone veneer, or even wood paneling. Real wood veneers or wood tongue-and-groove paneling come prefinished or ready for the color or stain of your choice. Construct a half-wall of glass blocks to provide privacy without completely closing off a space. Glass-block walls will allow light to stream from one room to another.

bright idea

let the sun shine in

Using glass doors in the basement will allow light to pass through adjoining areas. French doors, for example, brighten a windowless space by borrowing sunlight from another room.

RIGHT An arched stucco ceiling and dramatic lighting add an exotic, subtly mysterious atmosphere to this basement entry.

IIIII **decorative doors welcome guests to a wine-cellar entry** III

OPPOSITE The pilasters flanking these impressive-looking doors add drama and elegance. The hinges and handles continue the theme.

LEFT A cultured-stone column complements the wood-plank ceiling and decorative door, lending a distinctly medieval feeling to this wine-room entrance.

BOTTOM LEFT An arched door topped off with a metal grille opens up the view of the wine cellar while creating an Old World atmosphere.

BOTTOM RIGHT French doors allow light to pour through into the rest of the space, while the textured glass provides a certain amount of privacy.

BELOW A graceful curved bar, enhanced with wainscot-ing, is illuminated with track lighting that echoes its shape. Natural light from the windows and under-cabinet lighting further brighten the space.

OPPOSITE Stone and rough-hewn paneling, beams, and columns combine to create a dramatic spot for tasting a favorite bottle of wine. The slate floor and coordinating windowsills enhance the rustic atmosphere.

bright idea
keep it dry

Use special moisture-resistant types of drywall in moist areas of the base-ment. Solid-wood paneling is more durable but expands and contracts with changes in moisture levels.

IIIII rough-hewn paneling and stone create drama IIII

▐▐▐▐▐ a special ceiling treatment lends a dramatic touch ▐▐▐

TOP LEFT Suspended ceilings are an easy and inexpensive option for absorbing sound while providing easy access to basement pipes and wiring.

TOP RIGHT Beams and trimwork on the ceiling coordinate dramtically with the dark woodwork and wainscoting in this basement entertainment area.

OPPOSITE The ceiling is one of the most interesting features of this basement, thanks to its intricate border, halogen spotlights, and the map pattern that is reflected from the mirror on the table.

bright idea

build in the charm

A bead-board ceiling lends charm and character to a space. Using precut 4x8-foot sheets is easier than installing the individual tongue-and-groove planks.

take cover

Beams, columns, and ductwork can be handsomely camouflaged with trimwork and paneling. You can conceal water and gas pipes with a drop ceiling. You can also add architectural interest and remove pipes from view by hiding them within the beams of a coffered ceiling. Columns and beams can be sheathed in a wooden box and finished off with bead-board and trim that blends in with the rest of the basement's decor.

IIIIIIIII add architectural interest with trim and paneling IIII

ABOVE The handsome woodwork on the coffered ceiling, walls, and columns lends a rich presence to this basement room.

I

RIGHT A ledge on the wall opposite the bar is a convenient spot to rest a drink when there's a crowd.

I

OPPOSITE TOP A half-wall visually connects the fireplace seating area with the entrance to this basement.

I

OPPOSITE BOTTOM Spectacular wood paneling on the wall of this basement entertainment room draws the eye toward the fireplace and flat-panel TV.

Many homeowners see their basement as a logical place to add a bathroom. Whether built in conjunction with a family room, home gym, or guest room, a bathroom is a convenience, and it increases the resale value of your home. Although the standard sink, shower or tub, and toilet provide function, why not make the bathroom special? In a basement, you needn't worry about the extra weight of a water-filled tub—the concrete floor can handle it. Consider installing a roomy soaking tub or whirlpool spa made of stone, a shower outfitted with steam and multiple showerheads, or a sauna.

Private Space

I an extra half bath I an additional full bath I lighting and ventilation I
I saunas I

A custom mirror that spans across one wall helps to visually expand the space in this half bath.

an extra half bath

A half bath can incorporate many of the amenities and style that you'll find in a full bath. In small spaces, a handsome pedestal sink can add elegance to a plain bathroom. A corner sink or wall-mounted basin saves even more space. Round toilets take up less room than their conventional oval counterparts. If possible, the door should swing into the room to avoid blocking the outside hallway. If the space is too small for this solution, consider a pocket door. Because it's the bathroom most often used by guests, a half bath is a chance to showcase style without sacrificing functionality. Emphasize architectural details by bringing in moldings and wall treatments from surrounding spaces. Splurge on hardwood, stone, or mosaic-tile floors, and give the walls a rich color or pattern. A freestanding table near the sink is an attractive way to display hand towels. Instead of a traditional medicine cabinet, an antique mirror adds style and eye appeal.

Think creatively about storage, especially if the half bath is very small. Install shelves, or use a three-tiered hanging basket for cosmetics, soaps, or extra hand towels. Use woven baskets to hold cleaning products and extra linens. Install hooks for towels and robes behind the door. A cabinet can be built into the corner for storage.

OPPOSITE A sink dropped into an antique-style wood table, metallic wallpaper, and a sunburst mirror add glamour to this half bath.

ABOVE Handsome coordinating prints, elegant wallcovering, and a classic wall sconce increase this half bath's style quotient.

RIGHT A pedestal sink, outfitted with a modern faucet, adds plenty of style while saving space in this half bath.

half-bath style

You can transform a drab, windowless space into a charming retreat. Choose a bold paint color or dramatic printed paper for the walls; carry these strong colors into the accessories and towels. Recessed lighting and well-placed sconces illuminate the toilet and sink areas. A large mirror over the sink will reflect all the light in the room and pick up color and pattern. Stencil or paint a mural on the largest open wall.

OPPOSITE TOP Stone half walls, eye-catching art-work, and an oversize mirror create an over-the-top ambiance that belies the small stature of this bath.

OPPOSITE BOTTOM, LEFT AND RIGHT In this Cape Cod-inspired bath, a storage basket keeps fluffy towels handy near the sink; white wainscoting, blue walls, and a shell-frame mirror lend a charming seaside flair.

RIGHT A leaded glass window and iron chandelier draw the eye upward, visually enlarging this bath.

BELOW Elegantly crafted sconces and an antique mirror provide ample light for grooming.

RIGHT This elegant vanity, flanked by wood-paneled cabinets, adds loads of storage to a second bath.

FAR RIGHT Baskets let air circulate and are a stylish way to hold extra towels.

BELOW This narrow drawer is perfectly fitted for cosmetics and brushes.

BOTTOM LEFT A wire rack attached to the inside of a cabinet holds grooming tools.

BOTTOM RIGHT AND OPPOSITE Glide-out drawers and shelves make storing and finding toiletries a cinch.

big storage ideas for extra half baths

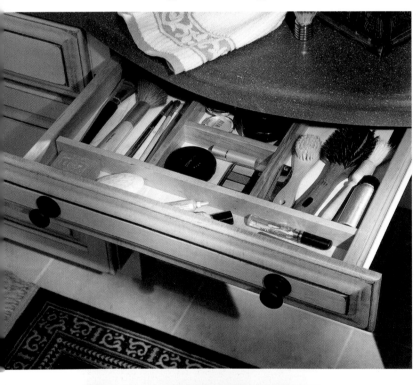

furniture-style vanities

A couple of years ago, an enterprising homeowner or interior designer came up with the idea of converting an antique washstand into a bathroom vanity, complete with sink and plumbing. The idea caught fire, and soon many homeowners were asking their decorators and contractors to duplicate this look. Furniture-like vanities not only add eccentric charm to the bathroom, but can sometimes provide more storage.

It wasn't long before bathroom cabinet manufacturers jumped on the bandwagon and began infusing their collections with crafted, glazed, distressed, and architecturally-ornamented vanities designed to look like antique washstands, chests of drawers, and tables. Taking the idea one step further, cabinet companies have now added coordinating wall cabinets, shelves, mirrors, and other storage pieces designed to harmonize with their furniture-like vanities. And while the bathroom furniture trend began with antiques, it has taken hold so firmly that contemporary pieces are now available for homeowners who prefer modern design.

bright idea

a smart fit

To be sure the faucet you like will flow at the perfect angle into the lav you've selected, buy them at the same time, preferably from the same retailer.

BELOW This his-and-her full bath offers the convenience of two grooming stations and built-in storage, along with the elegance and space-saving features of the pedestal sinks.

OPPOSITE If you can, position a tub underneath a bank of windows to provide both natural light and ventilation.

an additional full bath

Adding a full bath is one of the best ways to increase the value of your home. Make it special. One popular trend these days is to compartmentalize various areas in the bathroom. A toilet room, where the fixture is contained in a separate compartment or partially enclosed by a half wall, is one example of this style.

Ceramic tile has always been the material of choice in a bathroom because it is impervious to water and offers so many design possibilities. Natural stone, particularly granite, has nudged out ceramic tile in popularity in recent years. When choosing paint for the walls, look for one that contains mildewcide. Eggshell, satin, or semigloss finishes resist moisture better than flat paint. When you shop for a toilet, you'll find two bowl styles: standard and elongated. Two inches longer than the standard models, elongated one-piece toilets are considered more comfortable and sanitary.

More homeowners are opting for soaking tubs these days. Similar in length to standard tubs, they are a roomy 42 inches wide. Today, you can find a bathtub with a built-in headrest at one end and other handy options, including drink holders. Whirlpool tubs add convenience and comfort. They come in all shapes and colors. Some high-end extras include colored underwater lights, sound systems, and television sets.

Like whirlpool tubs, showers can now be outfitted with steam, multiple massage jets, or even video and audio equipment. A shower can be designed to be separate from the tub or to take the place of the tub altogether. If you don't like to take long baths, this can be a viable option for your home.

big **i**deas for **b**aths

Another space- and money-saving option is a standard-size whirlpool. However, if you prefer showers and rarely take a bath, eliminate the tub, especially if there is one in another bathroom in the house. Instead, install a larger shower, one with a roomy seat for two, built-in storage nooks, and perhaps a spa feature, such as massage jets or a rainbar. Don't overlook annexing a foot or two from an adjacent closet hallway or another room, or bumping out an outside wall a few feet over the foundation. Sometimes it's possible to position a fixture, such as a sink, a shower, or even a toilet, at an angle, which conserves space and, if planned properly, doesn't require long plumbing lines.

OPPOSITE Natural materials such as wood and stone add warm appeal to this modern whirlpool tub.

BOTTOM LEFT Water-resistant ceramic tile in a retro pattern is picked up in this large shower with bench seat.

BOTTOM RIGHT A neutral color pairing adds sleekness and serenity to this modern full bath.

A good lighting plan involves a series of layers. It starts by placing ample light where it is needed for bathing or grooming, and adds other light sources to enhance the overall mood of the room. Vanity lighting is especially important because these fixtures affect how you appear in the mirror and the ease with which you can groom. Side fixtures, such as sconces or vertical light bars, are solutions. When sidelights are impractical and you have to use an overhead fixture, install it 75 to 80 inches above the floor. In general, you will need at least 150 watts for grooming. Fixtures come in all types to match specific architectural and decorative styles.

lighting and ventilation

Proper ventilation should be part of any bathroom design. Bathroom fans usher damaging moisture and odors to the outside. Look for an exhaust fan that can move a lot of air (measured in cubic feet per minute, or cfm) without making a lot of noise (measured in sones). Make sure to put the fan on a separate switch so that you don't have to turn it on every time you flick on the light.

RIGHT Frameless glass shower doors visually enhance the size of this bathroom.

lighting for mirrors

You'll need even, shadow-free lighting for applying makeup, shaving, or grooming hair. It should illuminate both sides of the face, under the chin, and the top of the head. Plan to use at least 120 incandescent watts. Never aim lighting directly into the mirror. Decorative sconces installed on either side of a small mirror at face height do the job nicely. Place them no higher than 60 inches above the floor and at least 28 inches—but not more than 60 inches—apart, unless you pair them with another vanity light source.

add drama by directing a spotlight at a favorite print

bright idea
safe lights

Lighting around the tub and shower area has to be bright enough for safety and grooming and sufficiently protected from moisture. Choose shielded fixtures, which eliminate glare. Shatter-resistant white acrylic diffusers are the first choice for safety.

OPPOSITE Flexible halogen lighting can be directed wherever you need it. The built-into-the-mirror fixture sits above the large stone sink.

BOTTOM LEFT The neutral wall and flooring provide a welcoming palette for the darker accents of the vanity, commode seat, and artwork.

BOTTOM RIGHT Shaded sconces add intimate lighting while blending in nicely with the large floral print wallpaper. The mirror seems to enlarge the space.

Who doesn't love heading to a sauna after a tough gym workout on the elliptical trainer or treadmill? It is a luxury many have dreamed about having in their own home. Installing a sauna in your basement is easier than you might think. Because they use dry heat, saunas don't require a water supply or drain. What's more, the electricity for the sauna can be tied directly into existing circuits.

The original Finnish sauna was a one-room log cabin heated with a woodstove. Today, there are multiple options limited only by your space and budget. Some saunas even incorporate softly-lit dressing rooms, massage rooms, and cold-water plunges.

saunas

Prefab units, both compact and grand, come with doors, paneled walls, sauna stove, and all hardware. Larger versions can even include a bar and a bedroom. Many saunas are made of the traditional cedar and provide a soothing fragrance when heated up. Infrared saunas heat the body directly rather than circulating hot air throughout the enclosure.

When installing a sauna, include ventilation to take care of any condensation that might build up on the outside of the unit, as well as extra insulation in the walls to provide maximum energy efficiency.

hot ideas

▌ **Remove jewelry, eyeglasses,** and contact lenses. All may conduct heat in the sauna and cause burns.

▌ **Don't sauna on a full stomach.** Allow a couple of hours between your sauna time and meals to digest.

▌ **Plan your time.** Some people like to sauna after exercise to soothe sore muscles. Others prefer to sauna at the end of the day to bring on sleep.

▌ **Vary the heat and length of stay.** Novices need to build up endurance. Children, for example, should stick their feet in a bucket of cool water to moderate the impact of the heat.

ABOVE This prefab sauna includes plenty of custom touches, such as soft lighting, a storage bin for towels, and a bedlike platform for lying back and allowing the heat to unknot tense muscles.
▌
RIGHT A sauna made of cedar not only looks handsome, but also provides a woodsy fragrance. This unit includes a built-in sound system so you can relax to your favorite music.

8

A basement is the perfect place to set up shop. First, there's not much remodeling involved because electricity and running water may already exist. Another advantage is the built-in temperature control of a basement space. It's typically cool even on hot days, and because the heated house stands above it, a basement is comfortable in the winter. A triangle layout is ideal for most workshops. For woodworking, lumber and power tools are placed at one corner, the workbench at the second corner, and a finishing station at the third. Ultimately, though, you'll want a layout that is comfortable and convenient for your needs.

Workshops

I making plans I workbenches I

I tool storage I

Devise a workshop layout that fits your needs. Here a simple, uncluttered workbench, with slotted shelves that can be adjusted as needed, leaves plenty of room for storage underneath.

bright idea

roll 'em on over

Storage cabinets on casters provide not only a second work surface but also the convenience of portability when needed.

ABOVE Although originally designed for garages, these built-in and rolling cabinets work in basements as well. This workshop layout combines lots of storage options and space to work on large projects. The overhead racks are a smart way to hold long pieces of lumber.

OPPOSITE Everything is within reach in this woodworking shop. Perforated cabinet doors hold tools and other frequently used items.

making plans

K eep your workshop bright by painting the walls a light color, or choose paneling in a light-color finish that will reflect natural and artificial light. If you have a concrete floor, two coats of concrete paint will hide ugly stains. Alternatively, you can cover the floor with comfortable rubber floor mats. Use solid doors wherever possible to muffle noise. Portable heaters will keep the shop warm in winter, and window fans or a portable air conditioner will cool down the shop in summer. Ambient lighting from a window, as well as from overhead sources is best. Add a portable lamp that is adjustable when you need extra illumination for detail work. Make sure there is enough electrical power devoted to the space. Install electrical receptacles around the room, spacing them 36 inches apart. You can never have too many of them.

choose workshop flooring that's easy on your feet

fan facts

The easiest way to ventilate your workshop is with a fan. These come in a large array of styles and sizes.

❚ **Industrial fans** can move large amounts of air and are good for a big space.

❚ **Exhaust fans** help vent fumes and stale air from the workshop to the outdoors.

❚ **Box fans** are inexpensive and portable. When placed in a window, they draw in fresh air or remove stale air.

❚ **Enclosed fans** in forced-air systems can work with in-line filters to remove dirty air and return filtered air into the workspace.

ABOVE Workbenches come in a variety of materials. Here, a hardwood countertop can stand up to a lot of abuse without losing its natural good looks.

❚

OPPOSITE TOP Give a lot of consideration to the flooring in a workshop. Rubber mats resist the occasional spill and can be easily removed and hosed down.

❚

OPPOSITE BOTTOM These days, manufacturers customize shelving to suit a variety of needs. Here, a magnetic strip keeps tools in place and in full view.

bright idea

hit the deck

A rubber or vinyl floor is not only soft on the feet but slip-resistant and easy to clean.

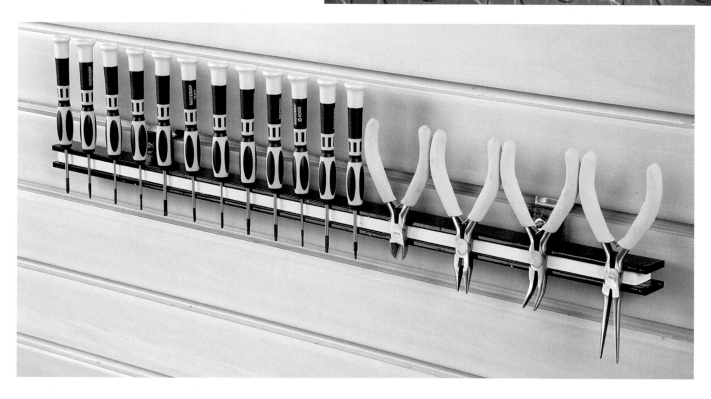

A workbench is an essential fixture for any job site or workshop. Portable or permanent, a bench not only helps you work faster and more accurately, it also keeps you safe. A portable workbench can be moved to wherever it is needed in the workshop. Many models have detachable casters and can be adjusted to varying heights. Some come with the option of a leveling mechanism or adjustable feet that allow you to keep your tools level or work on uneven surfaces.

Portable workbenches are designed to serve as a shop bench, router station, or clamping station. A stationary workbench is a sturdy alternative to a portable bench. It should measure at least 2 × 5 feet, and can cost anywhere from $100 to $1000 or more. The better models include drawers and cabinets. A stationary bench can be located in the middle

workbenches

of the shop so you can walk around it, or up against a wall for general storage and projects. A folding workbench is ideal when workshop space is at a premium. This type of workbench offers easy storage and a stable, broad base. Many models come with a tabletop clamping device to secure work to the table. Sawhorses can provide the base for a decent portable work surface. Foldable sawhorses made of aluminum, steel, or plastic are easy to store when you don't need them.

I I I I I I I everything within easy reach I I I I I I I

OPPOSITE LEFT This work-bench unit comes with storage cabinets that fit neatly under-neath the work surface.

OPPOSITE RIGHT Installing slotted shelves on a wall allows you to hold all kinds of tools and to rearrange them as needed.

RIGHT Using rubber or felt lin-ers prevents tools from moving around when you open or close the drawers of your workbench.

storage

Drawing each tool's outline on the surface where it is kept is a classic and efficient way to keep track of where each tool belongs on the wall (or inside a tool cabinet). Spotting an unfilled outline will quickly tell you when a tool is missing. Here are a few more helpful hints for creating smart storage:

❚ **Store large power tools** on a wall rack to keep them handy but out of the way.

❚ **Free up floor space**—and avoid tripping—by installing a wall rack for the ladder.

❚ **Keep hazardous materials** in a locked storage cabinet.

BELOW Simple perforated board and hooks hold a variety of tools, while a wood shelf adds extra storage for bulkier items used only on occasion.
❚

OPPOSITE A cabinet on casters is not only portable, but it can be outfitted with hooks to keep items within easy reach when working on a project.

tool storage

Adjustable, wall-mounted shelving is a staple for workshops. You can simply alter the height of your shelves as your needs change. Rolling cabinet carts can also be moved around to suit your needs. Equipment carts made of metal or plastic come with wheels and can hold heavy items in one compact unit. Perforated hardboard panels can be installed directly over or instead of wallboard.

Group similar tools together so you can find them quickly. Simple features, such as drawer dividers, will keep small items from becoming lost, and a rubber liner can prevent tools from sliding around when drawers are opened and closed. With everything neatly in place, you can focus on your projects and enjoy your workshop space without unnecesary distractions.

These days, when grandma lives in another city and teens are itching for more independence, many families must find creative ways to spend more quality time together. Sometimes, the solution for this can be right below your feet. A basement can be adapted to accommodate the needs of several generations of loved ones. If teenagers clamor for a place to call their own, you can meet them halfway by transforming your basement into their own semiprivate living space. Similarly, visiting relatives can get their fill of family time while knowing they can retreat to their own private haven for much-needed peace and quiet.

Making It Home

▌ light + warmth ▌ cozy kitchens ▌
▌ relaxation ▌

This elegant basement "mother-in-law" suite pulls out all the stops, with rich details such as wallcovering, wood floors, crown moldings, and gleaming lamps and accessories.

Before you embark on a basement renovation that involves additional living quarters, make sure to check with your local building inspector about the zoning regulations in your area. For example, some communities prohibit renting out a basement apartment, but do allow occupation by a relative or guest—which is how the term "mother-in-law suite" was coined. When designed carefully, these basement quarters can also work well for a live-in nanny or college-age children returning home during the holidays, or as a well-appointed guest retreat.

No matter who will spend the most time in this lower-level abode, you will want it to be cozy and inviting. For real comfort, there should be at least one bedroom; a sitting area; a small kitchen, kitchenette, or breakfast bar; adequate storage space; and

light + warmth

a full or half bath. (See "Private Spaces," Chapter 7, beginning on page 124.)

Lighting is also critical in a basement, where natural light is often at a premium. Coordinating all of your artificial lighting sources—lamps, recessed or track lighting, sconces, ceiling-mounted fixtures, and pendants—can make the difference between a place that is warm and welcoming or one that is dark and gloomy. Also remember that light has the power to visually reconfigure a space, making your belowground rooms seem larger, for example. Make sure to include adequate task lighting in the bathroom for grooming and one or two bedside lamps for reading.

If your basement is blessed with windows, you'll need to both enhance and control natural light. For example, you might want to cover a bedroom window in layers. A sheer curtain will provide filtered light; blackout-lined draperies will protect late sleepers from direct sun on lazy mornings.

LEFT Neutral walls and flooring make this compact basement retreat appear more spacious. The narrow bank of windows floods the space with natural light.

OPPOSITE This unstained pine platform bed and simple, slatted wall treatment give this downstairs bedroom a contemporary feel. The lamps and bedding add bright pops of color.

bright idea

sneeze stoppers

Carpeting and upholstery can harbor allergens. Keep clutter to a minimum; vacuum the room often; and use bedding with anti-allergen casings.

bed styles

The style of bed you choose can quickly transform the room. Some have both a headboard and a footboard, while others may have just a headboard or a frame. Here are some different types.

▌**Sleigh beds.** With a headboard and footboard that curve upward and resemble an old-fashioned sleigh, sleigh beds work well in rooms with low ceiling heights.

▌**Four-poster beds.** The posts can have elaborate finials or decorative additions. When a canopy is attached, this is called a tester. Unlike the sleigh bed, some four-posters may be extremely tall and work well only in bedrooms with high ceilings.

▌**Brass/iron beds.** Some antique metal beds can be quite elaborate and provide an instant touch of charm to a bedroom. However, they are uncomfortable to use if you like to sit up and read in bed.

▌**Upholstered beds.** An upholstered headboard and footboard are very comfortable if you sit in your bed to read or watch television.

▌**Trundle beds.** Instead of a box spring supporting a mattress, the bed is made up of a mattress that is supported by a frame. Under this structure is housed another bed that be reached by simply pulling it out from underneath the main bed. Trundle beds provide additional sleeping space when needed.

▌**Platform beds.** A mattress is placed on a wooden platform that provides the support for the sleeper. The platform can house various drawers, cupboards, and cabinets for clothing, linen, and accessory storage. The headboard is often flanked with bookcases and built-in night tables. Platform beds are perfect when storage is at a premium.

▌**Murphy beds.** Named for its designer, the Murphy bed folds up into an armoire, a wall unit, or even a closet when not in use.

OPPOSITE This bedroom has been designed into a basement nook. The four-poster beds add a homey touch to the space.

▌
ABOVE These slatted shelves give the room an uncluttered look. They can be rearranged to suit changing needs.

bright idea

lighten the tone

If your basement is short on natural light, use bright paint or glass blocks to create a sense of warmth and to reflect, transmit, and "amplify" available light.

LEFT This modern snack counter incorporates both storage and amenities. A glass-block wall adds light without sacrificing privacy.

ABOVE This composite countertop resembles granite but is easy to clean, resists scratches, and harmonizes with the stone-tile backsplash.

the two biggest-ticket kitchen items

cozy kitchens

Whether you are creating a second full-time kitchen or a less ambitious kitchenette, there are lots of ways to make the space both functional and beautiful. Before getting started, check with your local building department to make sure that adding a second kitchen to your basement is legal. If you get the go-ahead, you'll probably need some design ideas to help you wisely plan your time and budget.

The two biggest-ticket kitchen items are cabinets and appliances. You can save money by buying stock cabinets and customizing them with a kit that contains pre-cut ornamental pieces with self-adhesive backing. Plastic-laminate cabinets are available in a variety of patterns and colors and can be refaced relatively inexpensively. Eco-friendly kitchen products and materials are available in an ever-growing range of styles and costs. Look for "green" cabinets and countertops made of recycled tile, quartz composite—even paper or hemp.

The choices in appliances have grown exponentially. Ovens and cooktops now offer more precise heat control and options, such as one continuous grate or sealed burners so that pots slide smoothly across the cooking surface. New oven technology combines the benefits of both microwave and convection within a single unit.

Even if you don't need another full-size kitchen, you should consider an extra refrigerator in your basement suite. A modular freezer or refrigerator drawer can be installed into a bank of cabinets or drawers, putting cold drinks and snacks just where guests need them.

are cabinets and appliances IIIIIIIIIIIIIIIIIIIIIIIIIIIIIIIIIIIIII

OPPOSITE TOP This galley kitchen and the adjoining laundry are equipped with full-size appliances.

OPPOSITE BOTTOM A step-down kitchen makes use of long basement walls to provide plenty of counter and storage space.

BELOW A combination kitchenette-laundry in this guest suite maximizes a small space with all the comforts of home.

RIGHT In this stunning basement kitchen, space is saved by locating stainless-steel appliances, wine racks, and beverage storage under the counters.

comfort & safety

The National Kitchen and Bath Association recommends the following tips when designing your kitchen:

▌ **Choose flooring** that is slip-resistant.

▌ **Make sure any glass** in cabinet doors is tempered.

▌ **Keep a fire extinguisher** handy at all times.

▌ **Provide ground-fault circuit interrupter (GFCI) protection** for all electrical outlets.

▌ **Install faucets** with antiscald devices.

▌ **Use clipped or radius corners** and curved or beveled edges on countertops.

▌ **Use proper lighting.** Never work in a poorly lit area.

▌ **Choose a cooktop or stove** with front or side controls. If you have to reach over a hot pot or burner to use a control, you can be scalded.

The main area of the basement suite is where guests and family members get to kick back and relax. If you plan to divide the basement between a kitchen area, gameroom, sitting area, or media room, consider using a built-in divider or several bookshelf units placed side by side to separate the space. If possible, keep the layout open. Support poles encased in prefabricated columns divide basement spaces quite stylishly. Plan furniture groupings to encourage both comfort and conversation, but don't crowd too much furniture in a small space, either. Leave enough room for walking around the furniture and for stretching out legs when seated. A coffee table is a must, providing space for books and snacks. If possible, include a height-adjustable table that adapts for card-playing, dining, or work on a laptop. Glass tabletops are not a great idea if young children are around.

relaxation

OPPOSITE Clusters of furniture and a bar make this basement a more intimate entertaining space.

ABOVE This basement room uses posts and a half wall to create snack and lounging areas.

bring in the **s**unshine

To brighten and increase the airiness of your basement, here are some design tricks to enhance the natural light, no matter how much you get.

▎ **Color.** Painting the walls a warm neutral or warm white and installing light-color carpet, vinyl, or wood flooring considerably amplify natural light.

▎ **Furnishings.** Wicker or rattan furniture or tables with glass tops, as well as other furnishings that are open and light friendly, add airiness and a free-flowing feeling to an otherwise drab space.

▎ **Reflective surfaces.** Install mirrors and other reflective materials that can bounce natural or artificial light back into a room.

|||||||||||||||||||||||||||||||| plan furniture groupings to encourage

BELOW An oversize wooden table resembling an antique trunk creates a large coffee table—with storage—that becomes the center of attention.

RIGHT Soft throw pillows and a diminutive antique table warm up this family room almost as much as the rustic fireplace.

basement suite style

Washable slipcovers. Many ready-made versions are affordable and come in a wide range of styles, colors, and prints that you can change with the season.

Plenty of pillows. Throw pillows make a room feel cozy, and pillows with removable, washable covers make easy-care accents.

Flexible furniture groupings. The centerpiece of family relaxation is often a major focal point such as a flat-screen TV or fireplace. Ottomans or chairs on casters can be pulled into use when extra seating is needed.

Versatile pieces. An antique trunk or storage ottoman can double as a small table for books, magazines, remote controls, and drinks.

comfort and conversation ||||||||||||||||||||||||||||||||||||||||||||

bright idea

tread softly

You'll want something soft underfoot in the space where guests will lounge and relax. Coordinate rugs and carpets by matching the colorways, and avoid combining two overly bold patterns.

BELOW You can easily create the feeling of an elegant hotel lounge in your basement with classic furniture, fabrics, and accessories.

OPPOSITE If you have the space, you can add a full dining room in a basement suite for family entertaining.

10

orking at home has become part of many people's lives, whether it's telecommuting one day a week, running a home business, or finishing up work that's brought home from the office. A separate space makes work more efficient, and there's no better place to locate a home office than in the basement. Away from the buzz of household activity, it's possible to hear yourself think. A basement offers ample space and privacy, as well as a separate entry for clients. However, there is a long list of organizational and design issues that you'll need to tackle. Here are some ideas for maximizing your home-office space.

Home Offices

I a place for business I
I illuminating ideas I savvy storage I

Modular cabinets and shelves help keep office essentials within easy reach, while a generous L-shaped work surface provides room for computing and spreading out paperwork.

If you like total privacy, make sure to carve out a home office away from rooms that might be noisy, such as a laundry room or hobby room with video-game consoles. Also consider adding extra insulation in the walls and ceiling to cut down on noise pollution. Sound-absorbing, wall-to-wall industrial carpet and a heavy wood door with a lock might complete the peace-and-quiet picture. If you're not bothered by a little household hubbub as you work, design your office in a semiopen space, using curvy glass-block partial walls that won't completely close you off from the sounds of family life.

a place for business

Light-colored walls or the overuse of mirrors in a basement home office will increase glare and, possibly, eyestrain. It's best to stick with warm neutrals or a color you like and wouldn't mind living with for a long period of time.

It's also a smart idea to add an extra circuit to isolate your computer and other office equipment from power to the rest of your house. Drawing too much power from one circuit can trip circuit breakers and possibly cause the loss of valuable information.

When shopping for a computer table or unit, look for models that provide large grommets for those extra yards of annoying wires. Cord control is extremely important to the aesthetics of your home office as well as to your safety. To eliminate the tangle of cords and cables on the floor, install an outlet or phone jack on top of your computer desk, or mount it on the side of a base cabinet.

OPPOSITE Artwork, photographs, and favorite mementos help to warm up and personalize the modern furnishings of this small but elegant home office.

BELOW This space uses long basement walls for floor-to-ceiling storage. The light-colored wood opens up the space and provides room for personal items. Office basics are stored behind doors.

bright idea
keep it neat

Keeping your desktop tidy helps you work more efficiently, especially when your basement office is used by more than one person.

office layouts

The size, shape, and number of desks and surfaces your work and associated equipment require largely determines the optimal layout of your office. As you design the space, think creatively—and take advantage of the basement's nooks and crannies. Here are some common office configurations:

▌**Parallel.** Extra work surfaces, such as a credenza to hold a fax machine or copier, can be placed either behind or in front of the main work desk.

▌**L-shape.** A secondary work surface is attached at a right angle to the main desk. This is especially useful when standard pen-and-paper deskwork is combined with the use of a desktop computer or laptop.

▌**U-shape.** A variation on the L-shape, this configuration features two secondary work surfaces at right angles to the main work area. U-shaped layouts have the same advantages as the L-shaped arrangement, only more so.

illuminating ideas

A well-lit home office is a must, but properly designed lighting can also enhance flexibility when you want to rearrange furniture. Ideally, you should have natural and artificial light illuminating your space. Don't place your computer monitor too close to a window or skylight because glare can cause eyestrain. Choose window treatments that can be adjusted during the day. Curtains with insulated backs, wood blinds, and shutters are all effective and attractive choices. If your space is windowless, create your own "sun" with full-spectrum lightbulbs that simulate natural light.

To provide sufficient ambient light, layer artificial light by using recessed spots or cove lighting around the ceiling. Wall sconces are a good choice for indirect lighting, but in a home office they take up wall space and may need rewiring should you change the layout.

Desk-mounted lamps or floor lamps provide adjustable task lighting. Remember to locate task lighting behind your shoulder and to the side of the work surface. Another option is a light bridge built into the workstation itself. Include ample receptacles to allow task lights to be plugged in close to your work surface without the need for extension cords. Dimmers let you easily adjust light levels for the task at hand. Low-voltage halogen bulbs or fluorescent bulbs are energy-efficient and will also cut down on heat.

Track lighting is perfect for lighting photos, artwork, diplomas, and business accreditations. The light fixtures slide along the track to direct light at new additions.

LEFT Under-cabinet lighting combined with a desktop lamp supplies task lighting where it is needed most—on the work surface.

OPPOSITE A decorative chandelier makes a stylish counterpoint to the rectangular worktable. The desk lamp is adjustable to fit individual needs.

contemporary fixtures add style

BELOW Custom cabinets not only look good, but they also make use of every square inch of space in the room.

OPPOSITE The ambient light from the ceiling spots supplements the sleek, twin-fixture lamp on this desk.

bright idea

dim the lights

With lighting installed on dimmers, you can dim lights ever so slightly to extend bulb life and save energy.

The rule of thumb regarding office storage is that everything needed to do the job should be comfortably within arm's reach. That leaves quite a lot of stuff that can be stored away. Custom cabinets are the most efficient type of storage because they use every square inch of space. A freestanding, preassembled closet organizer for supplies and files,

savvy storage

or stock kitchen cabinetry featuring rollout drawers, lazy Susans, and other space-saving features are two lower-cost storage solutions. Or you can get creative: hang files in an old trunk, or store office supplies in clear plastic stacking cubes or modules.

Storage units can be intrusive, so if space is tight, consider recessing them into a wall or bumping them into an adjacent space. Use odd-shaped basement spaces to best advantage. Consider pullout storage drawers under the stairs, or add a half wall between basement columns to house bookshelves on the bottom and a spacious counter on top.

Extra supplies and outdated files can be kept in another space—perhaps a large walk-in closet. To prevent damage to stored items from excess moisture, be sure the space is air-conditioned, and install a dehumidifier.

The new generation of workstations accommodates large monitors and provides room for peripherals such as a CD burner, scanner, and additional hard drives. Some units contain ample storage for printer and fax paper, as well as small office supplies. Choose a unit with a locking mechanism for keyboard trays that pull out for those times when you have to remind yourself to get down to business.

LEFT Today's home-office storage solutions, such as this modern credenza in a dark finish, create high style without sacrificing function.

OPPOSITE TOP Store items you use occasionally in overhead cabinets, and keep current work in drawers within arm's reach.

OPPOSITE BOTTOM In this custom-built cabinetry, cubbies near the ceiling display personal collections.

ABOVE This custom built-in home office solution yields ample cabinets, cubbies, drawers, and open shelving for items both big and small.

RIGHT This wooden wall cabinet includes a fold-down charging station for cell phones and other electronic devices. Receptacles are hidden behind the shelf.

BELOW This European-style console, which boasts chrome hardware, translucent blue shelving, and under-cabinet lighting, serves as both office storage and a sleek cocktail bar.

RIGHT This combination of a tall armoire and matching low chest provide loads of storage for stacks of paper and other bulky items.

bright idea

stack it up

Think vertical when planning for storage. A floor-to-ceiling bookshelf, with doors or drawers at its base, is the most efficient configuration.

LEFT The lighthearted design of this home office welcomes budding executives. A chalkboard-painted wall and height-appropriate bulletin boards encourage creativity.

bright idea

keep it low

Use low-pile industrial carpet rather than a plusher weave to smooth the transition of rolling desk chairs and other portable equipment from one area to another.

OPPOSITE Laminate cabinetry in a neutral tone smartly contrasts with black drawers and pulls. The creative arrangement definitely catches the eye.

ABOVE An inexpensive desktop organizer keep supplies organized. It can be easily moved to fit your changing needs.

RIGHT This transparent file keeper is lightweight and stackable.

pain-free computing

Camping out in front of a computer can be a pain in the neck, wrist, eyes, hips...you get the picture. Here are some tips to take the ouch out of prolonged stints at the computer.

▌**Buy an adjustable chair** with a five-wheel base. The front of the chair should tip or tilt forward slightly to give you proper legroom. At a minimum, the chair should be curved at the front so as not to cut off the circulation in your legs.

▌**You should be about an arm's length away** from the monitor screen when you're sitting back in the chair. Your eyes should be level with an imaginary line that is about 2 or 3 inches below the top of the monitor.

▌**When word processing,** keep your wrists in a neutral (straight) position and your elbows at a 90-degree or greater angle. Use a light touch when typing (don't bang the keys), and don't use wrist rests and armrests when you're typing, only when resting.

▌**Change posture and activities often.** Variety is one of the most important preventive measures. Try to take a break even before you feel fatigued. Follow the 20-20-20 rule: take a 20-second break every 20 minutes and focus on a point at least 20 feet away to give your eyes a rest and a change of view. It's also good to get up from your chair every 30 minutes, move around, and do a few light stretches.

LEFT This compact home office cleverly fits all kinds of storage into a very a small space.

▌

OPPOSITE A translucent glass desktop, white cabinetry, and wall-mounted cabinets give a light, airy feel to this home workspace.

Resource Guide

MANUFACTURERS

Above View
414-744-7118
www.aboveview.com
Makes ornamental ceiling tiles.

Adagio, Inc.
www.adagiosinks.com
877-988-2297
Makes hand-crafted sinks in a variety of materials.

All Multimedia Storage
866-603-1700
www.allmultimediastorage.com
Manufactures media storage.

Amana
800-843-0304
www.amana.com
Manufactures refrigerators, dishwashers, and cooking appliances.

American Standard
www.americanstandard-us.com
Manufactures plumbing and tile products.

Amtico International Inc.
404-267-1900
www.amtico.com
Manufactures vinyl flooring.

Ann Sacks Tile & Stone, a div. of Kohler
800-278-8453
www.annsacks.com
Manufactures ceramic, glass, and stone tile.

Architectural Products by Outwater
800-835-4400
www.outwater.com
Manufactures hardwood and plastic moldings, niches, frames, hardware, and other architectural products.

Armstrong World Industries
717-397-0611
www.armstrong.com
Manufactures floors, cabinets, ceilings, and ceramic tiles.

Artemide
631-694 9292
www.artemide.com
Manufactures lighting fixtures.

Atlas Homewares
818-240-3500
www.atlashomewares.com
Manufactures house numbers, door knockers, and doorbells.

Bach Faucets
866-863-6584
www.bachfaucet.com
Manufactures faucets.

Ballard Designs
800-536-7551
www.ballarddesigns.com
An online and catalog source for decorative accessories, including boxes and baskets.

Baltic Leisure
800-441-7147
www.balticleisure.com
Manufactures steam showers and saunas.

Bassett Furniture Industries
276-629-6000
www.bassettfurniture.com
Manufactures both upholstered furniture and casegoods.

Bemis Manufacturing Co.
800-558-7651
www.bemismfg.com
Manufactures toilet seats.

Benjamin Moore & Co.
www.benjaminmoore.com
Manufactures paint.

Blue Mountain Wallcoverings, Inc.
866-563-9872

This list of manufacturers and associations is meant to be a general guide to additional industry and product-related sources. It is not intended as a listing of products and manufacturers represented by the photographs in this book.

www.imp-wall.com
Manufactures wallcoverings under the brand names Imperial, Sunworthy, Katzenbach & Warren, and Sanitas.

Brewster Wallcovering Co.
781-963-4800
www.brewsterwallcovering.com
Manufactures wallpaper, fabrics, and borders in many patterns and styles.

Calico Corners
800-213-6366
www.calicocorners.com
A national retailer specializing in fabric. In-store services include design consultation and custom window-treatment fabrication.

California Closets
800-274-6754
www.californiaclosets.com
Manufactures closet systems.

Central Fireplace
800-248-4681
www.centralfireplace.com
Manufactures freestanding and zero-clearance fireplaces.

CoCaLo, Inc.
714-434-7200
Manufactures juvenile bedding under the brand names CoCaLo, Oshkosh B' Gosh, Baby Martex, and Kimberly Grant.

Colebrook Conservatories
800-356-2749
www.colebrookconservatories.com
Designs, builds, and installs fine conservatories, glass enclosures, period glass structures, roof lanterns, and horticultural greenhouses.

Comfortex Window Fashions
800-843-4151
www.comfortex.com
Manufactures custom window treatments, including sheer and pleated shades, wood shutters, and blinds. Its Web site provides company information and a store locator.

Congoleum Corp.
800-274-3266
www.congoleum.com
Manufactures tiles and plastic-laminate flooring.

Country Curtains
800-456-0321
www.countrycurtains.com
A national retailer and on-line source for ready-made curtains, draperies, shades, blinds, hardware, and accessories.

Crossville, Inc.
931-484-2110
www.crossvilleinc.com
Manufactures porcelain, stone, and metal tile.

Couristan, Inc.
800-223-6186
www.couristan.com
Manufactures natural and synthetic carpets and rugs.

Dex Studios
404-753-0600
www.dexstudios.com
Creates custom concrete sinks, tubs, and countertops.

EGS Electrical Group
Easy Heat
860-653-1600
www.easyheat.com
Manufactures floor-warming systems.

Resource Guide

Elfa
www.elfa.com
Manufactures storage products.

Elkay
630-574-8484
www.elkayusa.com
Manufactures sinks, faucets, and countertops.

Ethan Allen Furniture
888-324-3571
www.ethanallen.com
Manufactures upholstered furniture and casegoods.

Expanko, Inc.
800-345-6202
www.expanko.com
Manufactures cork and rubber flooring.

Finn + Hattie, a div. of Maine Cottage
207-846-9166
www.finnandhattie.com
Manufactures juvenile furniture.

Finnleo
800-346-6536
www.finnleo.com
Manufactures saunas, steam baths, and accessories.

Fisher & Paykel, Inc.
888-936-7872
www.fisherpaykel.com
Manufactures kitchen appliances.

Florida Tile
800-242-9042
www.floridatile.com
Distributor and manufacturer of ceramic wall and floor tile.

Formica Corporation
513-786-3525
www.formica.com
Manufactures plastic laminate and solid surfacing.

Gautier
954-975-3303
www.gautierusa.com
Manufactures furniture.

General Electric
580-634-0151
www.ge.com
Manufactures appliances and electronics.

Ginger
www.gingerco.com
Manufactures lighting and bathroom accessories.

Glidden
800-454-3336
www.glidden.com
Manufactures paint.

Globus Cork
718-742-7264
www.corkfloor.com
Manufactures cork flooring.

Green Mountain Soapstone Corp.
802-468-5636
www.greenmountainsoapstone.com
Manufactures soapstone floors, walls, sinks, and countertops.

Haier America
877-337-3639
www.haieramerica.com
Manufactures electronics and appliances, including wine cellars.

Häfele America Co.
1-800-423-3531
www.hafeleonline.com
Manufactures cabinet hardware.

Hartco Hardwood Floors
800-769-8528
www.hartcoflooring.com
Manufactures engineered hardwood and solid-wood flooring.

Herbeau Creations of America
239-417-5368
www.herbeau.com
Makes vitreous china fixtures.

Hoesch Design
www.hoesch.de
Manufactures tubs and shower partitions.

Hunter Douglas, Inc.
800-789-0331
www.hunterdouglas.com
Manufactures shades, blinds, and shutters. Its Web site directs you to designers, dealers, and installers.

Ikea
www.ikea.com
Manufactures furniture and home-organization accessories.

Jacuzzi Inc.
800-288-4002
www.jacuzzi.com
Manufactures spas and shower systems.

Jenn-Air, a div. of Maytag Corp.
Maytag Customer Service
800-688-1100
www.jennair.com
Manufactures kitchen appliances.

Jian & Ling Bamboo
757-368-2060
www.jianlingbamboo.com
Manufactures vertical and horizontal cut bamboo flooring.

Kemiko Concrete Products
903-587-3708
www.kemiko.com
Manufactures acid stains for concrete flooring and other concrete products. Creates decorative concrete floors.

KidKraft
800-933-0771
www.kidkraft.com
Manufactures children's furniture.

Kirsch Window Fashions
800-538-6567
www.kirsch.com
Manufactures blinds, rods, shades, and holdbacks.

Kohler
800-456-4537
www.kohler.com
Manufactures plumbing products.

Kraftmaid Cabinetry
440-632-5333
www.kraftmaid.com
Manufactures cabinetry.

Resource Guide

Lambs and Ivy
800-345-2627
www.lambsandivy.com
Manufactures juvenile bedding, rugs, lamps, and accessories.

Lane Home Furnishings
www.lanefurniture.com
Manufactures both upholstered furniture and casegoods.

Laticrete International, Inc.
203-393-0010
800-243-4788
www.laticrete.com
Manufactures epoxy grout in many colors.

La-Z-Boy
www.la-z-boy.com
Manufactures furniture.

LG
800-243-0000
www.lge.com
Manufactures major appliances.

Lightology
866-954-4489
www.lightology.com
Manufactures lighting fixtures.

Maytag Corp.
800-688-9900
www.maytag.com
Manufactures major appliances.

Merillat
www.merillat.com
Manufactures cabinets.

MGS Progetti
www.mgsprogetti.com
Manufactures stainless-steel faucets.

Moen
800-289-6636
www.moen.com
Manufactures plumbing products.

Motif Designs
800-431-2424
www.motif-designs.com
Manufactures furniture, fabrics, and wallcoverings.

Neo-Metro, a div. of Acorn Engineering Co.
800-591-9050
www.neo-metro.com
Manufactures countertops, tubs, lavs, and tile.

Nuheat Industries, Ltd.
800-778-WARM
www.nuheat.com
Manufactures radiant electric floor heating systems.

NuTone, Inc.
888-336-3948
www.nutone.com
Manufactures ventilation fans, medicine cabinets, and lighting fixtures.

Osram-Sylvania
978-777-1900
www.sylvania.com
Manufactures lighting products and accessories.

PatchKraft
800-866-2229
www.patchkraft.com
Manufactures coordinated bedding for cribs and twin- and full-size beds, using infant-safe fabrics.

Plaid Industries
800-842-4197
www.plaidonline.com
Manufactures stencils, stamps, and craft paints.

Plain and Fancy Custom Cabinetry
800-447-9006
www.plainfancycabinetry.com
Makes custom cabinetry.

Precor USA
800-786-8404
www.precor.com

Manufactures cardiovascular fitness equipment, such as elliptical trainers, for residential and commercial use.

Price Pfister, Inc.
800-732-8238
www.pricepfister.com
Manufactures faucets.

Remcraft Lighting Products
www.remcraft.com
Manufactures lighting fixtures.

Restoration Hardware
800-910-9836
www.restorationhardware.com
Manufactures indoor and outdoor furniture, windows, and lighting accessories.

Robern, a div. of Kohler
www.robern.com
Manufactures medicine cabinets.

Schonbek Worldwide Lighting Inc.
800-836-1892
www.schonbek.com
Manufactures crystal lighting fixtures.

Seabrook Wallcoverings, Inc.
800-238-9152
www.seabrookwallpaper.com
Manufactures borders and wallcoverings.

Seagull Lighting Products, Inc.
856-764-0500
www.seagulllighting.com
Manufactures lighting fixtures.

Sharp
www.sharpusa.com
Manufactures consumer electronics.

Sherwin-Williams
www.sherwinwilliams.com
Manufactures paint.

Spiegel
Spiegel Customer Satisfaction
800-474-5555
www.spiegel.com
An on-line and paper catalog source of all types of window treatments, hardware, and related embellishments.

Resource Guide

Springs Industries, Inc.
888-926-7888
www.springs.com
Manufactures window treatments, including blinds and shutters, and distributes Graber Hardware.

Sonoma Cast Stone
888-807-4234
www.sonomastone.com
Designs and builds concrete sinks and countertops.

Stanley Furniture
276-627-2100
www.stanley.com
Manufactures entertainment centers and other home furniture.

Stencil Ease
800-334-1776
www.stencilease.com
Manufactures laser-cut stencils and related tools and supplies.

Stickley Furniture
315-682-5500
www.stickley.com
Manufactures furniture.

Sub-Zero Freezer Co.
800-222-7820
www.subzero.com
Manufactures professional-style refrigeration appliances.

Sure-Fit, Inc.
888-754-7166
www.surefit.com
Manufactures ready-made slipcovers and pillows.

Tarkett
www.tarkett-floors.com
Manufactures vinyl, laminate, tile, and wood flooring.

Thibaut Inc.
800-223-0704
www.thibautdesign.com
Manufactures wallpaper and fabrics.

Thomasville Furniture Industries
800-225-0265
www.thomasville.com
Manufactures wood and upholstered furniture and casegoods.

Toto USA
770-282-8686
www.totousa.com
Manufactures toilets, bidets, sinks, and bathtubs.

Viking Range Corp.
www.vikingrange.com
Manufactures professional-style kitchen appliances.

Villeroy and Boch
877-505-5350
www.villeroy-boch.com
Manufactures fixtures, fittings, and furniture.

WarmaTowel, a div. of Sussman
800-667-8372
www.nortesco.com/sussman/towel/towel.html
Manufactures towel-warming metal racks.

Warmly Yours
800-875-5285
www.warmlyyours.com
Manufactures radiant floor heating systems.

Watermark Designs, Ltd.
800-842-7277
www.watermark-designs.com
Manufactures faucets and lighting fixtures.

Waterworks
800-998-2284
www.waterworks.com
Manufactures plumbing products.

Waverly Baby
800-423-5881
www.waverly.com
Manufactures bedding, wallcoverings, and window treatments for the nursery.

Whirlpool Corp.
www.whirlpool.com
Manufactures home appliances and related products, including a drying cabinet and an ironing center.

Wilsonart International
800-433-3222
www.wilsonart.com
Manufactures plastic laminate countertops.

Wolf Appliance Company
www.wolfappliance.com
Manufactures professional-style cooking appliances.

Wood-Mode Fine Custom Cabinetry
877-635-7500
www.wood-mode.com
Manufactures custom cabinetry.

York Wallcoverings
717-846-4456
www.yorkwall.com
Manufactures borders and wallcoverings.

ASSOCIATIONS

National Association of Remodeling Industry (NARI)
800-611-6274
www.nari.org
A professional organization for remodelers, contractors, and design-build professionals.

National Kitchen and Bath Association (NKBA)
800-652-2776
www.nkba.org
A national trade organization for kitchen and bath design professionals, offering consumers product information and a referral service.

Glossary

Accent Lighting: A type of lighting that highlights an area or object to emphasize that aspect of a room's character.

Accessible Designs: Those that accommodate persons with physical disabilities.

Adaptable Designs: Those that can be easily changed to accommodate a person with disabilities.

Analogous Scheme: See Harmonious Color Scheme.

Ambient Lighting: General illumination that surrounds a room. There is no visible source of the light.

Art Deco: A decorative style that was based on geometric forms. It was popular during the 1920s and 1930s.

Art Nouveau: A late-nineteenth-century decorative style that was based on natural forms. It was the first style to reject historical references and create its own design vocabulary, which included stylized curved details.

Arts and Crafts Movement: A decorative style that began in England during the late nineteenth century, where it was known as the Aesthetic Movement. Lead by William Morris, the movement rejected industrialization and encouraged fine craftsmanship and simplicity in design.

Backlighting: Illumination coming from a source behind or at the side of an object.

Backsplash: The vertical part at the rear and sides of a countertop that protects the adjacent wall.

Box Pleat: A double pleat, underneath which the edges fold toward each other.

Broadloom: A wide loom for weaving carpeting that is 54 inches wide or more.

Built-In: Any element, such as a bookcase or cabinetry, that is built into a wall or an existing frame.

Cabriole: A double-curve or reverse S-shaped furniture leg that leads down to an elaborate foot (usually a ball-and-claw type).

Candlepower: The luminous intensity of a beam of light (total luminous flux) in a particular direction, measured in units called candelas.

Casegoods: A piece of furniture used for storage, including cabinets, dressers, and desks.

Clearance: The amount of space between two fixtures, the centerlines of two fixtures, or a fixture and an obstacle, such as a wall.

Code: A locally or nationally enforced mandate regarding structural design, materials, plumbing, or electrical systems that state what you can or cannot do when you build or remodel.

Colonial Style: An early-American architectural and decorative style started during the Colonial period and influenced by design ideas brought by settlers from Europe, particularly England.

Color Wheel: A pie-shaped diagram showing the range and relationships of pigment and dye colors.

Complementary Colors: Hues directly opposite each other on the color wheel. As the strongest contrasts, complements tend to intensify each other.

Contemporary: Any modern design (after 1920) that does not contain traditional elements.

Cove: 1. A built-in recess in a wall or ceiling that conceals an indirect light source. 2. A concave recessed molding that is usually found where the wall meets the ceiling or floor.

Daybed: A bed made up to appear as a sofa. It usually has a frame that consists of a headboard, a footboard, and a sideboard along the back.

Dimmer Switch: A switch that can vary the intensity of the light it controls.

Distressed Finish: A decorative paint technique in which the final paint coat is sanded and battered to produce an aged appearance.

Dovetail: A joinery method in which wedge-shaped parts are interlocked to form a tight bond. This joint is commonly used in furniture making.

Dowel: A short cylinder, made of wood, metal, or plastic, that fits into corresponding holes bored in two pieces of wood, creating a joint.

Faux Finish: A decorative paint technique that imitates a pattern found in nature.

Federal: An architectural and decorative style popular in America during the early nineteenth century, featuring delicate ornamentation and symmetrically arranged rooms.

Fittings: The plumbing devices that bring water to the fixtures, such as faucets.

Fluorescent Lighting: A glass tube coated on the interior with phosphor, a chemical compound that emits light when activated by ultraviolet energy. Air in the tube is replaced with a combination of argon gas and a small amount of mercury.

Focal Point: The dominant element in a room or design, usually the first to catch your eye.

Footcandle: A unit that is used to measure brightness. A footcandle is equal to one lumen per square foot of surface.

Framed Cabinet: A cabinet with a full frame across the face of the cabinet box.

Frameless Cabinet: A cabinet without a face frame. It may also be called a "European-style" cabinet.

Frieze: A horizontal band at the top of the wall or just below the cornice.

Full-Spectrum Light: Light that contains the full range of wavelengths that can be found in daylight, including invisible radiation at the end of each visible spectrum.

Gateleg Table: A drop-leaf table supported by a gate-like leg that folds or swings out.

Georgian: An architectural and decorative style popular in America during the late eighteenth century, with rooms characterized by the use of paneling and other woodwork, and bold colors.

Gothic Revival: An architectural and decorative style popular during the mid-nineteenth century. It romanticized the design vocabulary of the medieval period, using elements such as pointed arches and trefoils (three-leaf motifs).

Greek Revival: An architectural and decorative style that drew inspiration from ancient Greek designs. It is characterized by the use of pediments and columns.

Ground-Fault Circuit Interrupter (GFCI): A safety circuit breaker that compares the amount of current entering a receptacle with the amount leaving. If there is a discrepancy of 0.005 volt, the GFCI breaks the circuit in a fraction of a second. GFCIs are required in damp areas of the house.

Grout: A mortar that is used to fill the spaces between tiles.

Glossary

Hardware: Wood, plastic, or metal plated trim found on the exterior of furniture, such as knobs, handles, and decorative trim.

Harmonious Color Scheme: Also called analogous, a combination focused on neighboring hues on the color wheel. The shared underlying color generally gives such schemes a coherent flow.

Hue: Another term for specific points on the pure, clear range of the color wheel.

Incandescent Lighting: A bulb (lamp) that converts electric power into light by passing electric current through a filament of tungsten wire.

Indirect Lighting: A more subdued type of lighting that is not head-on, but rather reflected against another surface such as a ceiling.

Inlay: A decoration, usually consisting of stained wood, metal, or mother-of-pearl, that is set into the surface of an object in a pattern and finished flush.

International Style: A post–World War II architectural and decorative style that emphasized simplicity and lacked ornamentation. Smooth surfaces, an extensive use of windows, and white walls are hallmarks of this pared-down style.

Lambrequin: Drapery that hangs from a shelf, such as a mantel, or covering the top of a window or a door. This term is sometimes used interchangeably with valance.

Love Seat: A sofa-like piece of furniture that consists of seating for two.

Lumen: The measurement of a source's light output—the quantity of visible light.

Lumens Per Watt (LPW): The ratio of the amount of light provided to the energy (watts) used to produce the light.

Modular: Units of a standard size, such as pieces of a sofa, that can be fitted together.

Molding: An architectural band used to trim a line where materials join or create a linear decoration. It is typically made of wood, plaster, or a polymer.

Mortise-and-Tenon Joinery: A hole (mortise) cut into a piece of wood that receives a projecting piece (tenon) to create a joint.

Neoclassic: Any revival of the ancient styles of Greece and Rome, particularly during the late eighteenth and early nineteenth centuries.

Occasional Piece: A small piece of furniture for incidental use, such as end tables.

Orientation: The placement of any object or space, such as a window, a door, or a room, and its relationship to the points on a compass.

Panel: A flat, rectangular piece of material that forms part of a wall, door, or cabinet. Typically made of wood, it is usually framed by a border and either raised or recessed.

Parquet: Inlaid woodwork arranged to form a geometric pattern. It consists of small blocks of wood, which are often stained in contrasting colors.

Pattern Matching: To align a repeating pattern when joining together two pieces of fabric.

Pediment: A triangular piece found over doors, windows, and occasionally mantles. It also refers to a low-pitched gable on the front of a building.

Peninsula: A countertop, with or without a base cabinet, that is connected at one end to a wall or another counter and extends outward, providing access on three sides.

Post-Modernism: A term used to define the developments in architecture and interior design that originated in modernism but began to diverge from that style. Unlike modernism, it includes ornamentation and uses historical references that are often whimsically out of context.

Primary Color: Red, blue, or yellow that can't be produced in pigments by mixing other colors. Primaries plus black and white, in turn, combine to make all the other hues.

Secondary Color: A mix of two primaries. The secondary colors are orange, green, and purple.

Sectional: Furniture made into separate pieces that coordinate with each other. The pieces can be arranged together as a large unit or independently.

Slipcover: A fabric or plastic cover that can be draped or tailored to fit over a piece of furniture.

Stud: A vertical support element made of wood or metal that is used in the construction of walls.

Task Lighting: Lighting that concentrates in specific areas for tasks, such as preparing food, applying makeup, reading, or doing crafts.

Tone: Degree of lightness or darkness of a color.

Tongue-and-Groove Joinery: A joinery technique in which a protruding end (tongue) fits into a recess (groove), locking the two pieces together.

Track Lighting: Lighting that utilizes a fixed band that supplies a current to movable light fixtures.

Trompe L'oeil: Literally meaning "fool the eye"; a painted mural in

which realistic images and the illusion of more space are created.

Tufting: The fabric of an upholstered piece or a mattress that is drawn tightly to secure the padding, creating regularly spaced indentations.

Turning: Wood that is cut on a lathe into a round object with a distinctive profile. Furniture legs, posts, rungs, etc., are usually made in this way.

Uplight: Also used to describe the lights themselves, this is actually the term for light that is directed upward toward the ceiling.

Valance: Short drapery that hangs along the top of a window, with or without a curtain underneath.

Value: In relation to a scale of grays ranging from black to white, this is the term to describe the lightness (tints) or darkness (shades) of a color.

Vanity: a bathroom floor cabinet that usually contains a sink and storage space.

Veneer: High-quality wood that is cut into very thin sheets for use as a surface material.

Wainscotting: A wallcovering of boards, plywood, or paneling that covers the lower section of an interior wall and usually contrasts with the wall surface above.

Welt: A cord, often covered by fabric, that is used as an elegant trim on cushions, slipcovers, etc.

Work Triangle: The area bounded by the lines that connect the sink, range, and refrigerator. A kitchen may have multiple work triangles. In an ideal triangle, the distances between appliances are from 4 to 9 feet.

Index

Index

Index

Photo Credits

All photos by Olson Photographic, LLC, unless otherwise noted.

page 1: design: Brindisi & Yaroscak page 3: Design: Hobbs page 4: design: Linda Lee Butler Interiors page 8: *top* design: RMS Construction; *bottom* design: Flanagan Interior Finish page 9: design: Amazing Spaces page 10: design: Putnam Kitchens page 12: design: Country Club Homes pages 14–15: *left* design: Caulfield & Ridgway; *center* deign: Amazing Spaces; *right* design: Avon Ridge pages 16–17: *all* design: Fairchild House Interiors pages 18–19: *all* courtesy of Whirlpool; *illustration* Stephen Fuller, Inc. pages 20–21: *left* design: CK Architects; *center & right* design: Amazing Spaces pages 22–23: *left* courtesy of California Closets; *top center* design: BRW and Associates; *bottom center* design: Avon Ridge; *right* design: Pembrooke/Caledon page 24: design: Benchmark Builders page 25: design: Peter Cadoux Architects pages 26–27: *left & center* design: JCK Interior Design; *top right* Phillip H. Ennis Photography, design: Robert DeCarlo; *bottom right* Phillip H. Ennis Photography, architect: Andrew Chary & Associates page 28: design: James Davis Architect page 30: *top* design: Frank Mairano Associates Inc.; *bottom* design: Brindisi & Yaroscak pages 32–33: *top center* design: Peter Cadoux Architects; *right* design: Kling Brothers Builders pages 34–35: *left & top right* design: Hobbs; *bottom right* design: Frank Mairano Associates Inc. page 36: *both* design: Peter Cadoux Architects pages 38–39: *left* design: Hallmark Woodworkers; *top & bottom right* design: RMS Construction page 40: design: Brindisi & Yaroscak page 41: *bottom* design: JCK Interior Design pages 48–49: *both* design: Peter Cadoux Architects pages 52–53: *all* design: Kling Brothers Builders pages 54–55: *all* design: EH Kitchens page 57: *right* design: White Architects page 58: design: James Davis Architects page 81: *top left* design: Peter Cadoux Architects; *top right* design: Callaway Wyeth/Timberdale Homes page 62: design: Turnkey Associates page 64: design: Richard Gordon Interests page 65: *top* design: Turnkey Associates; *bottom* design: Pembrooke/Caledon page 66: design: Pembrooke/Caledon page 67:

design: Linda Lee Butler Interiors pages 68–69: *both* courtesy of Armstrong page 70: design: Laurent T. DuPont, AIA page 71: *top* courtesy of Mannington; *bottom* design: InnerSpace Electronics Inc. pages 72–73: *both* courtesy of California Closets pages 74–75: *both* design: Sally Scott Interiors page 76: *top* courtesy of Hearth & Home page 77: design: Sally Scott Interiors page 78: design: Hallmark Woodworkers pages 80–81: design: EH Kitchens page 82: *top right* design: Hobbs; *bottom* design: Brindisi & Yaroscak page 83: design: Hobbs pages 86–87: *all* design: Peter Cadoux Architects pages 88–89: *all* design: Eric Strachan Custom Homes page 92: *top* design: Kitchen & Bath Designs By Betsy House pages 94–95: *all* design: Putnam Kitchens pages 98–99: *top center & top right* design: Peter Cadoux Architects pages 100–101: *all* design: Hallmark Woodworkers page 102: design: Peter Cadoux Architects page 104: *right* design: McWilliam-Autore Interiors; *right* design: Amazing Spaces pages 106–107: *top left* design: Coastal Point Construction; *bottom left & right* design: Olga Adler Interiors page 108: *left* design: Sellars-Lathrop Architects; *right* Peter Cadoux Architects page 109: design: the Designer Heritage page 110: design: Laurent T. DuPont, AIA page 111: design: Brindisi & Yaroscak pages 112–113: design: Kling Brothers Builders page 116: design: Kling Brothers Builders page 117: *bottom left* design: Peter Cadoux Architects; *right* design: Kling Brothers Builders page 118: design: Pembrooke/Caledon page 119: design: Hallmark Woodworkers page 120: *top left* design: BRW & Associates; *top right* design: Kling Brothers Builders page 121: Phillip H. Ennis Photography, design: Lucretia Moroni, Ltd pages 122–123: *top both* design: InnerSpace Electronics Inc.; *bottom both* design: Hallmark Woodworkers page 124: design: Brindisi & Yaroscak page 127: *left* design: McWilliam-Autore Interiors page 128: *left & bottom right* design: Artful Sinks; *top right* design: Amazing Spaces page 129: *both* design: Benchmark Builders pages 130–131: *top center, bottom center, bottom left & top left* courtesy of Merillat; *bottom right & center left* courtesy of Kraft-Maid pages 132–133: *both* design: Avon

Ridge page 134: design: Laurent T. DuPont page 135: *right* design: RMS Construction page 137: design: Coastal Point Construction page 138: design: Brindisi & Yaroscak page 139: *left* design: JCK Interior Design; *right* design: Sally Scott Interiors page 140: courtesy of Finnleo page 141: Phillip H. Ennis Photography, design: Greenbaum Interiors/Lynne Cone pages 142–143: *both* courtesy of Gladiator/Whirlpool page 145: Kenneth Rice page 146: courtesy of Gladiator/Whirlpool page 147: *top* courtesy of Flexco; *bottom* design courtesy of Gladiator/Whirlpool pages 148–149: *all* courtesy of Gladiator/Whirlpool page 150: John Parsekian/CH page 151: courtesy of Gladiator/Whirlpool page 152: design: Nest of Southport page 154: design: Robik Glantzz Builders page 155: courtesy of IKEA page 156: design: Hemingway Construction page 157: courtesy of IKEA page 158: *left* design: Complete Construction; *right* courtesy of Osram-Sylvania page 160: *top* design: Peter Cadoux Architects page 161: *right* design: RMS Construction; *left* Sellars-Lathrop Architects page 163: design: Complete Construction page 164: design Olga Adler Interiors pages 166–167: design: RMS Construction page 168: courtesy of Merillat pages 170–171: *both* courtesy of IKEA page 173: design: Kitchen & Bath Designs By Betsy House page 174: design: Kling Brothers Building page 175: courtesy of IKEA page 176: design: Laurent T. DuPont, AIA page 177: Phillip H. Ennis Photography, design: Richard Mishaan Designs page 178: courtesy of ALNO page 179: *top* courtesy of California Closets; *bottom* design: Laurent T. DuPont, AIA page 180: *top* design: Flanagan Interior Finish; *bottom* courtesy of Improvements Catalog page 181: *left* courtesy of ALNO; *right* courtesy of IKEA page 182: courtesy of IKEA page 184: courtesy of Crystal Cabinet Works page 185: *both* courtesy of Rubbermaid pages 186–187: *both* courtesy of IKEA page 189: design: RMS Construction page 190: design: Peter Cadoux Architects page 192: courtesy of Osram-Sylvania page 194: design: Peter Cadoux Architects page 196: design: Coastal Point Construction page 199: Laurent T. DuPont Interiors page 203: design: Peter Cadoux Architects page 206: design: Hobbs

Have a home gardening, decorating, or improvement project?
Look for these and other fine **Creative Homeowner** books wherever books are sold

Design Ideas for Kitchens provides design inspiration for creating an attractive, up-to-date kitchen. Contains hundreds of photographs and a wealth of information.

Over 500 photographs.
224 pp.
$ 19.95 (US)
$ 21.95 (CAN)
BOOK #: CH279412

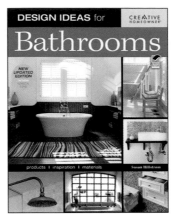

Design Ideas for Bathrooms offers hundreds of color photographs and extensive information on the latest trends in design, materials, and related products.

Over 500 photographs.
224 pp.
$ 19.95 (US)
$ 21.95 (CAN)
BOOK #: CH279261

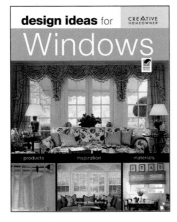

Design Ideas for Windows prodvides hundreds of window treatment images and ideas for every room.

Over 400 photographs.
256 pp.
$ 21.95 (US)
$ 25.95 (CAN)
BOOK #: CH279376

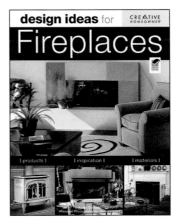

Design Ideas for Fireplaces provides a showcase for today's best hearth appliances for both inside the house and outdoors on a porch, patio, or deck.

Over 400 photographs.
208 pp.
$ 19.95 (US)
$ 24.95 (CAN)
BOOK #: CH279709

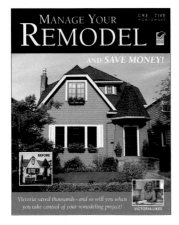

Manage Your Remodel — And Save Money gives tips and advice on how to be the general contractor on a large-scale remodel.

Over 220 photographs.
192 pp.
$ 16.95 (US)
$ 20.95 (CAN)
BOOK #: CH277874

Paint Saves the Day provides inspiration and step-by-step instructions to transform your everyday items using paint.

Over 275 photographs.
208 pp.
$ 19.95 (US)
$ 23.95 (CAN)
BOOK #: CH279575

For more information and to order direct, go to **www.creativehomeowner.com**